Their War
The Perspectives of the South Vietnamese Military in the Words of Veteran-Émigrés

Julie Pham, PhD

DEDICATION

To those who have continuously fought for freedom, democracy, and human rights.

To my father, Kim Pham, and to all those who served in the South Vietnamese military.

CONTENTS

ACKNOWLEDGMENTS

To the librarians at the Indochina Center at UC Berkeley and the Vietnam Center and Archives at Texas Tech University for patiently helping a young scholar.

To the Haas Scholars Program for financially supporting this original research and for providing me with a community of like-minded undergraduate researchers.

To my professors at University of California, Berkeley for teaching me to question the perspectives from which history is written. Special thanks to my honors thesis advisor, Professor Peter Zinoman.

To my father, Kim Pham, and all of his friends, colleagues, and South Vietnamese military veterans who agreed to share their stories for this work.

INTRODUCTION

When I first began my research two years ago, I remember riding in the car with two men I was about to interview on their experiences in the Republic of Vietnam Armed Forces (RVNAF). One man said to the other, "Bạn không bao giờ tìm thấy những bài viết về Quân Đội Việt Nam Cộng Hòa trong lãnh vực truyền thông Hoa Kỳ như họ đã dành cho Cộng Sản Việt Nam." His friend retorted, "Lý do có như vậy bởi vì chúng ta là kẻ thua trận."[1] Their words intrigued me then as they intrigue me now because they forced me to ask: How are the RVNAF portrayed in American representations? How do we understand who they are in the context of the Vietnam War? And what does that say about how we understand the Vietnam War in general? Do they see themselves as losers, and if not, how do they deal with the Americans who do see them that way? How

---

[1] Translated by Kim Pham. The conversation took place March 27, 1999. The first man is Bao Quoc Pham, who says: You never see articles written on the ARVN in the American press like they have on the communists. The other man, Con Gia Pham, says in response: That's because we're the losers.

much has being in America changed the way they look at the war? How do they remember the war? Through my research, I discovered that many of the South Vietnamese military veterans I interviewed had the same sense about their place in America now as these two men, that the RVNAF had not just lost the war, but also their place in the history of the war.

In this historiographical and historical study, I pose two research questions. First, how have the RVNAF come to be understood in American representations? I examined depictions of the South Vietnamese military in their relationship to the American military in postwar American film and literature. My analysis pinpointed tropes repeatedly used to characterize the RVNAF: apathy, incompetence, and corruption. In order to try to understand the Vietnam War, American writers and filmmakers often categorize the participants as the winners and the losers. This strategy then cast the Americans as the "losers" and relegate the South Vietnamese to being their sidekicks. Ironically, the real "losers," the South Vietnamese military, are only defined in relation to the other two parties. Compared to the North Vietnamese, they are the Westernized sell-outs who couldn't even fight and to the Americans, they are their "Vietnamese surrogates," as Neil Sheehan describes them. In the postwar representations, the relationship between the Americans and the South Vietnamese is underpinned by a paternalizer-subordinate dichotomy.

In the second part of my study, I ask how the veterans I interviewed see themselves in relation to those tropes and how they remember their role in the war. When I first began interviewing, I assumed that the RVNAF were subordinates to the Americans, and I admit I expected to hear testimonies denouncing paternalistic Americans — what I discovered was much different. Many of veterans revealed that they did not feel they were fighting a proxy war, that they were equal allies to the Americans, and that the tropes were in some ways true and in some ways false. At the same time, I took into account their émigré status when I gauged what their stories could tell me about what happened. From my interviews, I began to doubt the premise of the tropes—the assumption of an American as paternalizer-RVNAF as subordinate relationship. I also questioned the functions of the tropes, realizing they were to define the RVNAF and to ultimately blame the South Vietnamese and the RVNAF for the loss of the war. Unlike the postwar representations I examined, my research agenda centers on the question of "what happened in Vietnam?" rather than "who do we blame for this loss?" I will argue that how these South Vietnamese military veterans react to these tropes and how they remember the war, the Americans, the Communists, and themselves does not necessarily revolve around defining themselves as subordinates to the Americans. As a departure from the typical "Vietnam story," these interviews with South Vietnamese veterans demonstrate the possibilities of remembering and reimagining the Vietnam War from different perspectives.

BACKGROUND

Officially, the Republic of Vietnam Armed Forces
(RVNAF) did not form until 1955 when the United States
turned Southern Vietnam into the Republic of Vietnam
(RVN). Before that, the French organized Vietnamese
into the Vietnamese National Army in 1950, in their
efforts to oust the Viet Minh. The Viet Minh would later
become the Vietnamese Communists (VC). In 1953, the
French began to "Vietnamize" their own military, marking
the first Vietnamization effort in the war. Under the
Geneva Agreements in 1954, Vietnam was divided into
North and South at the 17th parallel. For one year, people
were allowed to move across that border; estimates of
800,000-1 million refugees moved from the North to the
South. When the United States set up the U.S. Military
Assistance Advisory Group (MAAG) in 1954, it had taken
over the training and equipping of these Vietnamese,
though the French continued to train the Vietnamese air
forces and navy until 1957.[2] Statistically, more than 30

---

[2] Lt. Gen. Dong Van Khuyen, *The RVNAF*, Indochina Monographs
(Washington, D.C.: U.S. Army Center of Military History, 1980), 2. There
are two spellings of "adviser"/advisor. As there is no consistency in the

percent of the South Vietnamese men were in uniform, from ages 18 to 45.[3] When the first American troops arrived in 1965, many Vietnamese had been fighting for up to 15 years. By 1969, there were 875,833 men in the RVNAF—the largest troops on either side of the war.[4] The Americans numbered 543,482, followed by the 236,800 men in the North Vietnamese/ Vietnamese Communists forces.[5] There was at least one RVNAF member in every South Vietnamese household.[6] American support for the RVNAF and the RVN had grown steadily since 1955 and in time, Lt. Col. Dong Van Khuyen wrote that the "Vietnamese army came to be totally dependent on U.S. ability to provide aid each year and on the U.S. concept of common defense."[7] Americans at home also supported the war until the 1968 Tet Offensive, which journalist Peter Braestrup argues was the definitive turning point in American public support. Antiwar protest on the domestic front helped push for American withdrawal from Vietnam.[8] The second Vietnamization began in 1969 and lasted until 1973, marked by the signing of the Paris Peace Accords between America and North Vietnam. When the war ended with the Fall of Saigon in 1975, RVNAF

Vietnam war literature, even across primary sources, I will use "advisor" unless it is quoted otherwise.

[3] "Building up the ARVN," *Time* 4 August 1967: 24-25.

[4] Khuyen, 22.

[5] Michael Clodfelter, *Vietnam in Military Statistics: A History of the Indochina Wars, 1772-1991* (Jefferson, NC; London: McFarland & Co., 1995), 151-152.

[6] Khuyen, 379.

[7] Ibid., 8.

[8] Peter Braestrup, Big Story: How the American Press and Television Reported and Interpreted the Crisis of Tet 1968 in Vietnam and Washington, abridged ed. (New Haven and London: Yale University Press, 1977).

officers were sent to reeducation camps. Estimates of the number of people sent range from 50,000 to more than 350,000.[9] Political dissidents, RVN civil servants, teachers, native Catholic clergy, among others, had also been sentenced to these camps. Vietnamese immigration has been ongoing since 1975, with scholars identifying as many as five waves.[10] This study will only deal with three broadly defined waves: first, those who left in 1975 after the fall of Saigon; 2) 1978-1989, refugees who escaped by boat or over land under the Orderly Departure Program (ODP) and 3) those who left after 1989, when the Comprehensive Plan of Action and Humanitarian Order (HO) was implemented.

---

[9] Marc Leepson with Helen Hannaford, eds., Dictionary of the Vietnam War (New York: Webster's New World (Simon & Schuster, 1999), 340.

[10] James M. Freeman, Changing Identities: Vietnamese Americans 1975-1995, New Immigrants Series, ed. Nacy Foner (Boston: Allyne and Bacon, 1995).

METHODOLOGY

Over the course of two years, I have conducted interviews with over 40 former RVNAF officers who now live in Seattle, Sacramento, San Jose, and Orange County, four of the five largest Vietnamese émigré communities in the United States, on their experiences in the RVNAF.[11] The interviews were usually conducted in English, though some interviews were done in Vietnamese with a translator, and some interviews were in English and Vietnamese without a translator. They lasted between 30 minutes and two and a half hours, and took place in various offices, the homes of the interviewees, and public places. While my question set adapted to what my subjects found most interesting, I usually asked about their personal background and early thoughts on the war, their wartime experiences, and then their postwar reflections. When I finished my interviewing entirely, I sent my informants a survey so that I may have answers to a consistent set of questions, including questions I formed later in my study. Thirty one out of 40 returned the survey.

---

[11] Bảo Quốc Phạm và Cổn Gia Phạm are residents of Orange Country. However, I interviewed both of them on 27 March 1999. All of the interviews have been edited for clarity.

I based the answer options to this multiple-choice survey on answers most often given to me during the interviews.[12]

I found my subjects through a network of friends and acquaintances, the "snowball method"; I talked to one person who referred me to another person, who then referred me to two or three more people, and so forth. As the daughter of a former naval officer and editor of a Vietnamese newspaper in Seattle, I had a relatively easy time accessing my informants. Because of my personal background, most of my subjects seemed to trust me. "I have been asked to give interviews about the war before," said Cam Nguyen told me before our interview, "but I didn't want to. Because you're Vietnamese though, I want to help."[13]

---

[12] I sometimes referred to the interview transcripts from people who I did not receive surveys from to find out what they would have answered in compiling my statistical data. Survey results in author's possession.

[13] Cam Nguyen, interview by author, San Jose, Calif., 7 August 2000. This is a pseudonym. See Appendix 1 for more background information on informants.

PERSONAL BACKGROUNDS OF
VETERANS-ÉMIGRÉS

Since I defined my informant group broadly, regular forces of the RVNAF, there was a multitude of differences in wartime and postwar experiences.[14] I have targeted three waves in which the men joined the war effort: 1950-62: low action; 1963-68: American involvement intensifies; and 1969-1972: Vietnamization. Fourteen men joined in the first wave, 11 men in the second, and 15 in the third. The men interviewed range in age from 44 to 72, with the average age at 58. Typically, the earlier a man joined the military, the higher his rank. These veterans ranged in rank from cadet officer to colonel, though most were captains and majors. The vast majority were from middle class socioeconomic backgrounds, with only three men identifying with "upperclass" and two "agricultural class." Although they all had the minimum of a high school education required of officers, many said their parents were not educated beyond high school. Forty-five percent of the veterans had some college education, and a handful had studied at the postgraduate level. In general, they were

---

[14] 31 men were in Army (ARVN); four in the Air Force, three in the Navy, and two in the Marine Corps.

more educated than the average South Vietnamese population; for example, all those who returned the survey noted they knew at least one foreign language before they enrolled in the RVNAF.[15] Most of the men interviewed were drafted, others volunteered, and then there were those who enlisted because they knew they would otherwise be drafted. Twenty three of the veterans were originally born in North Vietnam and moved with their families to the South in the 1950s, usually during the 1954 exodus.

The diversity of the veterans' postwar experiences is also important to understanding their different interpretations of the war. Those of the first immigration wave in my sample group tended to be among the Vietnamese elite: the higher ranking officers and those with connections to Americans who warned them to leave Vietnam. Many have since been able to achieve middle-class to upper-middle class prosperity in the United States. The second wave mimics the first wave in resettlement patterns. Unlike the first wave, however, most of these second wave émigrés had gone to reeducation camp. Upon their release, they felt compelled to escape the country because they feared that they would be forced to return to reeducation camp or saw no future for their children in Vietnam or both. Everyone in the third wave had gone to reeducation camp, spending an average of 8.4 years there. Because of their age, their language limitations, and their recent arrival status, the majority of those third wave immigrants I interviewed have yet to achieve the same level of economic prosperity and integration into mainstream American culture as those in the first and second waves nor do they necessarily want to. For reasons I will discuss later, the majority of the men I interviewed immigrated in the third wave, with only 10 percent of the men in the second wave and 32.5 percent in

---

[15] Survey results.

the first wave.[16]

---

[16] Survey results. See Appendix 2 and 3 for "Waves of Immigration" and "Years in Reeducation Camp" charts.

METHOD OF ANALYSIS

"On the deepest level, the legacy of Vietnam is the disruption of our story, of our explanation of the past and vision of the future." said John Hallmann.[17] The story Hallmann refers to is that of continual American victory and moral heroism. In understanding the Vietnam War as a "disruption," it is not surprising that postwar American representations of the South Vietnamese-American alliance center on the question: Who is to blame for the loss of the war? The initial answers usually point to the Americans, either the left-wing interpretations that "We never should have been there in the first place" or the right-wing view that "We did not do all we could do to win this war."[18] With the former, the Vietnam War is considered a neoimperial project and Americans were guilty of getting involved in a war they should have avoided. With the

---

[17] qt.. in Andrew Victor Martin, "Critical Approaches to American culutral STudies: The Vietnam War in Hisotry, Literature, and Film" (Ph.D. diss., U Iowa, 1987), 188.

[18] For a detailed intepretation of Vietnam War historiography, see Gary R. Hess, "The Unending Debate: Historians and hte Vietnam War," *Diplomatic History* 18, no. 2 (1994): 239-264.

latter, the Americans still consider themselves responsible for the victory of the war; they failed by not putting forth full military effort. Both these arguments assume that Vietnam was a proxy war and that American paternalism blinded the United States into thinking that they could win when, as former Secretary of State Robert McNamara said, "if the South Vietnamese were to be saved, they had to win the war themselves."[19] Based on the assumption of American paternalism, we can interpret the U.S.-RVN relationship as hostile and antagonistic; the South Vietnamese resent being subordinates and the Americans resent carrying the burden of the war.

The Americans can be faulted on these two counts, but postwar representations absolve them of guilt by ultimately blaming their partners, the South Vietnamese. I have identified three tropes used in postwar representations that blame the loss of the war on the RVNAF: apathy, incompetence, and corruption. But these tropes do not just function to fault the RVNAF; they also define the RVNAF. The RVNAF does not exist outside its role as subordinate and scapegoat to the Americans.

The postwar representations I examined interprets the U.S.-RVN relationships at all levels of power. I conducted interviews with officers, the middle echelon of the RVNAF, and the relationships they described are usually with their middle-echelon American equivalents, advisors. This study of the South Vietnamese military perspective is limited to officers, who arguably experienced the most intimate level of American-South Vietnamese relations. As a Vietnamese general said, "At the middle echelons the difficulties in interaction were greatest, the personalities involved being no longer candid and disinterested, and yet not completely mature in judgments and attitudes."[20]

---

[19] Robert McNamara, *In Retrospect: The Tragedy and Lessons of Vietnam* (New York: Vintage Books, 1996), 333, emphasis in original.

[20] op. cited in Stephen T. Hosmer, Konrad Kellen, and Brian M. Jenkins, *The*

Since the fighting battalions were not integrated, Vietnamese and American grunts had no significant daily contact with one another. As for the high ranking officials, a consensus exists among those I interviewed as well as numerous secondary sources that Americans did assume the control in the decision-making with their Vietnamese counterparts. The RVNAF perspective through officers allows a particularly insightful look into American-South Vietnamese relationship.

How postwar representations depict the RVNAF is embedded in how they view American paternalism and how they approach the study of the war. I argue that how these RVNAF veterans interpret these tropes reveals a different interpretation of the U.S.-RVN alliance and a different personal agenda in remembering the war. I examined 1) the attitudes toward the tropes describing the RVNAF; 2) the assumption of American paternalism; and 3) the need to blame in postwar representations and in RVNAF reinterpretations.

Fall of South Vietnam: Statements by Vietnamese Military and Civilian Leaders (New York: Crane, Russak and co, Inc. 1980), 82-83. The general is unnamed.

POSTWAR REPRESENTATIONS

Inserted between battle scenes of Stanley Kubrick's Full Metal Jacket[21] is a makeshift documentary featuring American GIs. Sergeant "Joker" asks each GI the question: "Does America belong in Vietnam?" They stand in front of tanks, bombed out buildings, or just in the middle of the field, wearing uniforms caked with dust and war worn; their expressions as they look into the camera range from serious concentration to nonchalant blankness. One by one, these fictional GIs express their thoughts; their words captured in bitesize clips: "Does America belong in Vietnam? I don't know, but I can tell you I belong in Vietnam"; "Can I quote LBJ? 'I will not send American boys 5,000 miles away to fight a war that Asian boys should be fighting themselves'(in a Texan drawl)"; "Personally don't think they really want to be involved in this war. It's sort of like they took away our freedom and gave it to the gookers. (laughs) They don't want it they rather be alive than free. Poor dumb bastards"; "I'm not real keen on some of these fellers who are supposedly on

21 *Full Metal Jacket*, dir. Stanley Kubrick, 118 min., Warner Brothers, 1987, videocassette.

our side. I keep meeting them coming the other way.'"
"We keep getting killed for all these people and they don't
even appreciate it. They think it's a big joke."; "If you ask
me, we shooting the wrong gooks." The South
Vietnamese are mentioned in only two other places in the
film: when Sergeant Rafterman, epitomizing American
nativity and blind patriotism, said: "You know what really
pisses me about these people? We're supposed to helping
these people and they shit all over us every chance they
get;" and when an ARVN officer acts as pimp, offering a
group of GIs the services of a young woman. These self-
consciously made clips combined comprise five minutes of
the film and within that short span of time, we learn the
RVNAF were apathetic, incompetent, and corrupt. The
Americans defined the RVNAF in comparison to
themselves: the Americans cared so much about freedom,
they were willing to sacrifice their own for others, and the
RVNAF did not care about freedom; the Americans, as we
can see in their attitudes and war worn postures that they
took the war seriously, and the South Vietnamese thought
it was a "big joke"; and the RVNAF are compared to the
North Vietnamese when Animal Mother comments that
the Americans are shooting the "wrong gooks." Not only
do the Americans define them, but we get the sense that
the Americans are fighting for them instead of with them.
These men do not consider the RVNAF their allies or
their equals in fighting for freedom. We are to understand
that any loss can be explained by the poor performance of
the South Vietnamese. Although this is an American film,
Kubrick is British, which makes the rendering of the GIs
an even more powerful critique of American paternalism.

Aside from Full Metal Jacket, I also looked at
Apocalypse Now (1979), and Good Morning, Vietnam
(1987). As for nonfictional accounts, I draw from Neil
Sheehan's Pulitzer Prize-winning biography of U.S.
Advisor Lieutenant Colonel John Paul Vann, A Bright
Shining Lie; and three popular textbooks on the Vietnam

War, George Herring's America's Longest War (1979), Marilyn Young's The Vietnam Wars, 1945-1990 (1990), and Robert Buzzanco's Vietnam and the Transformation of American Life (1999).[22] Because no major American postwar representations focuses on the RVNAF, I looked to these sources as popular examples that even mention the RVNAF at all to argue their depictions of the Vietnamese reflect dominant consensus in American historiography of the war.

Although the perception of the RVNAF as subordinates to the Americans is consistent in both wartime and postwar representations, the support for the American effort in the war has shifted from liberal righteousness preserving the Cold War mentality to liberal guilt toward the North Vietnamese people. Lost during that shift are whatever nuances that existed in explaining the RVNAF's negative reputation. On one level, American writers blame the loss of the war on the nation's own paternalism that initiated this neoimperial effort. But they also blame the RVN and the RVNAF. By shifting the

---

[22] *Apocalyse Now*, dir. Francis Ford Coppola, 150 min., United Artists, 1979, videocassette; *Good Morning, Vietnam*, dir. Barry Levinson, 116 min., Buena Vista, 1987, videocassette; Neil Sheehan, *A Bright Shining Lie* (New York: Vintage Books, 1988), this was a national bestseller; George Herring, *America's Longest War: The United States and Vietnam, 1950-1975*. (New York: Knopf, 1979); Marilyn Young, *The Vietnam Wars, 1945-1990* (New York: HarperCollins, 1991). Robert Buzzanco. *Vietnam and the Transformation of American Life*. in Problems in American History (2). Jack P. Greene (ed). (Malden, Mass.; London: Blackwell Publishers, 1999). Herring's work is said to be "one of the most widely used of the available texts,...readable, soundly documented, and provides a balanced interpretation." (Joe P. Dunn, *Teaching the Vietnam War: Resources and Assessments*. Occasional Paper Series No. 18, Los Angeles: Center for the Study of Armament and Disarmament, 1990. Udo Heyn, Ed. p. 17. The essay is written in 1990, too soon to assess Young's book. However, cultural historian Tomas Sandoval said, "Every standard class on the Vietnam War, unless they have a problem with her politics, uses Young." As for Buzzanco, this is his second book on the Vietnam War. His first work, *Masters of War: Military Dissent and Politics in the Vietnam Era* (1996) received the Stuart L. Bernath Prize for best book of 1996 in diplomatic history, which attests to his position as a respected authority on the Vietnam War.

ultimate blame to the RVNAF, Americans can absolve themselves of guilt.

Along with the need to blame, American resentment over the loss of the war also reinforces the need for these tropes. We see how the GIs in Full Metal Jacket feel that their freedom is taken away to fight in a war that the South Vietnamese should be fighting. Only one scene in Good Morning, Vietnam shows an American officer and a RVN soldier interact; the American burst out in anger and yells, "Listen jerko, we're here fighting for your country" in resentment and frustration. Not only do the Americans resent doing what they feel is the brunt of the work, they also resent working with the "wrong gooks," those who are not nearly as patriotic or competent as the ones they are fighting.

In a battlefield scene in Apocalypse Now, a VC soldier is lying in a dirt ditch. Surrounding him are a few American GIs and an ARVN soldier. Colonel Kilgore (Robert Duvall), who epitomizes American arrogance, sees the man and barks out, "Hey, hey, what's this?" "This man is hurt pretty bad, sir," a GI replies. "About the only thing holding his guts in is that pot lid." Kilgore turns to the ARVN soldier and demands, "What do you have to say?" The ARVN soldier, clad in a similar attire to that of the GIs, replies, "He is dirty VC. He wants water. He can drink paddy water." Colonel Kilgore pushes the South Vietnamese soldier away and yells, "Get out of here...get out of here before I kick your fucking ass." "He killing our people!" the ARVN soldier yells back. Grabbing his canteen, Kilgore says, "Any man brave enough to fight with his guts hanging out can drink from my canteen any day" and starts to pour the water down the VC's open mouth. This particular scene reflects the assumptions made about the South Vietnamese and the war in general in postwar representations: 1) how the Vietnam war is seen as being fought between the Americans and the Communists, with the South Vietnamese pushed to the side; 2) the subordinate status of the ARVN soldier to Americans when his words were completely ignored; and 3) how the Americans perceive the Communists as braver fighters who were willing to die, unlike the ARVN soldier in his clean, pressed uniform. By portraying the Communists as ruthless, diehard patriots, the film implies that Communists are willing to sacrifice their lives for their cause, and that the VC are more authentically Vietnamese than the Westernized sidekick of the Americans.

These tropes and assumptions also resonate in the written text. A Bright Shining Lie is journalist Neil Sheehan's biography of John Paul Vann, a man who represented the "one clear-sighted participant in an enterprise riddled with arrogance and self-deception" who later "embraced the follies he decried," he thought the war had been won.[23] Vann represents the arrogant and patriarchal attitude of Americans in this war and toward their Vietnamese allies.[24] Once, during a battle, Vann bullied his counterpart, Ba, which only "increased Ba's resistance. "Although their relationship was usually 'bluff and easy,' sometimes Vann could become "overbearing." "Ba had come, out of his pride, to resent the superiority complex of these Americans," wrote Sheehan, and that day, Ba found Vann to be "singularly grating." But Ba did not know:

"the pent-up emotions that were the larger source of Vann's abusive language and the extent to which Vann was in turn a prisoner of the American system. In the U.S.

---

[23] Quotes are from book cover. For more discussion of how the RVNAF are represented in this book, see Nguyen Manh Hung, "Journalistic Distortion: Neil Sheehan's Portrait of the Vietnesme in *A Bright Shining Lie* (1988)," *Journal of Vietnam Veterans Institute* 2, no.1 (1993): 17-31.

[24] Sheehan personally worked with Vann, when he was a young journalist and Vann was one of the few American advisors that the press corp felt they could believe. For more, read William Prochnau, *Once Upon a Distant War* (New York: Times Books, 1995), 60.

army, when a combat emergency occurred and a senior officer took charge, he issued brisk orders and everyone obeyed instantly. Vann could not help reverting to this procedure in his current predicament."[25]

Understandably, Sheehan focuses on Vann's frustrations and his doubts that the American advisors could turn the "ARVN into an army capable of fighting and winning the war against its guerrilla opponent."[26] But Sheehan assumes the way to understand the RVNAF mentality in the American-RVNAF relationship is to sympathize with their "resistance" to an overbearing attitude. This resistance is what we call the expected response from a subordinate who revolts against his superior. At the same time, he excuses Vann's frustration with the incompetence of his counterpart by attributing it to cultural differences: Americans believe in efficiency; the Vietnamese apparently do not. Like in the other postwar representations, Sheehan manages to criticize the Americans for their paternalism while blaming the RVNAF.

The tropes described thus far define the RVNAF explicitly against their allies and implicitly against their enemies, the North Vietnamese. The South Vietnamese only exists as subordinates to the Americans. The textbook writers invoke more explicit comparisons between the apathetic, unpatriotic RVNAF and the "diehard" Vietnamese Communists, with the exception of Herring, who limits his discussion of the RVNAF to a few short and dry sentences. Since Herring is the most influential of all three, the absence of the RVNAF from Herring's work is an indicator of their status in the general history of the war. In Young's work, the VC are what the

[25] Sheehan, 234.

[26] Ibid., 94.

RVNAF are not, the RVNAF are what the VC are not. Young assumes that the Vietnam War was a neocolonial project, that the RVNAF are victims of that project. She sympathizes with the RVNAF as subordinates to the Americans, but sees the VC as the authentic Vietnamese, and the RVNAF as the "foreign native." In one of the many anecdotes, Young describes how a village celebrated the establishment of the National Liberation Front by flying 600 homemade NLF flags. The villagers protested when ARVN soldiers tried to remove them, arguing that "This is a flag of peace. It is not a VC flag. This flag means that the people, some of whom are your relatives or even your families, have land to till."[27] The charming story illustrates Vietnamese sympathy for the VC. Young's narrative, however, has not even attempted to be balanced by also integrating success stories of ARVN pacification efforts in the strategic hamlet program.

Furthermore, Young said that the VC "control virtually all facets of peasant life in the southernmost provinces and the government troops there are reduced to defending the administrative centers."[28] Not only are the VC more persuasive recruiters, but they are more attuned to the lives of the Vietnamese villagers—they are more authentically "Vietnamese." This tenet clearly emerges in Young's discussion of the Tet Offensive of 1968, which was a military victory for the ARVN and American side and a psychological victory for the VC.[29] Of the two interpretations, Young concentrates on the latter, detailing how the guerillas were able to move into the city, "mingling easily with the crowds visiting relatives for the Tet holiday, hiding in the homes of sympathizers."

---

[27] qtd. in Young, 85-86.

[28] Young, 109.

[29] See Braestrup, who shows how the press depicted it as a very hard earned victory and shows how the VC aren't done yet.

Despite criticizing the NLF for its inability to "protect" the villagers, Young nonetheless suggests a close, friendly relationship between the Vietnamese Communists— one that the ARVN do not share with the civilians. She ends the passage on a note of sympathy for the VC, that the loss of so many of them was "deeply felt."

Young who often disguises her own opinions by citing those who she agrees with and omitting those who she disagrees with. Unlike Young, Buzzanco's admiration for the VC is evident in his own commentary. Instead of comparing the VC to the RVNAF, though, Buzzanco glorifies the VC and suggests the American military should have modeled them in discipline, strategy, and morale. He sees war is between the Communists and the Americans. He does not define the ARVN against the VC because he barely mentions the ARVN, though when he does mention them, his description of them is like that of the other two scholars. He oddly treats the American GIs as drug-addicts while attributing communists victories to their patriotism and will to fight. Indeed, the common perception of the Vietnamese Communists is consistently positive in comparison to both the Americans and the ARVN. Buzzanco entitles one section of his book "Charlie Meets G.I. Joe," indicative of how he categorizes the military participants. When he supports those "peasant nationalists living in an underdeveloped Asian nation," he refers to the Vietnamese Communists rather than the Southern Vietnamese noncommunist forces who also sought independence.[30] Young and Buzzanco's emphasis on the Vietnamese Communist help reinforce the assumption that the RVNAF were subordinates to the Americans, that they served the Americans while the VC served the Vietnamese people.

These postwar representations employ dichotomies to describe the South Vietnamese in relation to the

---

[30] Buzzanco, 14.

Americans and to the North Vietnamese. The veterans themselves questioned and challenged the very foundation of these descriptions.

INTERPRETATIONS BY THE VETERANS

The veterans' memories are not just reflections of what happened during the war, but of their own lives in America now. In the United States, Vietnamese émigrés, particularly RVNAF veterans, are distinct from other émigré groups in that they represent living reminders of a war that America lost and that it is still trying to understand why it lost. When the first waves of Vietnamese refugees came in 1975, they were met with much resentment and bitterness, especially in the context of a sluggish economy.[31] Their candidness often depends on how much they have integrated into mainstream American culture. However, I stress that my sample group is too small to draw definitive patterns; the veterans' postwar experiences do not always correlate with certain interpretations of the past. "[Americans] think I am a boat people and possibly, a loser, but I am not upset," said Can

[31] Julie Pham, Klara Schneider, and Sandy Xie, "Examination of the First, Third, and Fifth Wave Perception and Reception by *The New York Times* and *The Los Angeles Times*." Term Paper. UC Berkeley. Fall 1999. In author's possession.

Tran, a first wave refugee and now a successful computer engineer. "Deep down they don't know much about what is going on." He feels less compelled to defend his role in the war effort, and in fact, he seldom talks about the war, even with his own children. He said that overall military experience was "nothing special, everyone had to do it." His reluctance to talk about the Vietnam war reflects the attitude of many of those who are more established in the mainstream American culture, and who feel less of a need to legitimate themselves to those Americans who may automatically and negatively associate them with the war. They seem less defensive about preserving a positive image of the RVNAF, less concerned with what Americans thought of them.

My study comprised mostly of third wave émigrés because they were more interested in talking. Compared to third-wavers, a greater percentage of those in the first and second wave were more hesitant to talk to me. In such cases, my connections finally convinced them to grant an interview. First- and second-wavers were less likely to respond with answers lined with anticommunist rhetoric. Because of their moderate position toward communism, they were more likely to use pseudonyms.[32] Can Tran explained, "We have to get over the war, but some people in San Jose don't like that idea, so don't use my real name."[33]

In contrast, 80 percent of the third wave granted permission to use their real names. For first and second-wave immigrants, they came at younger ages and still felt that it was worthwhile to make efforts at assimilating into

---

[32] Four out of five first wave immigrants and two out of five second wave immigrants chose to use pseudonyms (survey results). I excluded the first 10 interviews conducted in Spring 1999 from this survey of who uses pseudonyms because I did not give informants a choice in the matter.

[33] Can Tran, interview by author, San Jose, Calif., 24 June 2000. This is a pseudonym.

mainstream society for the benefit of their children. Those who came in the third wave were usually in their 50s and 60s, a much more difficult age to reestablish oneself in the same way as a man who immigrates in his 30s or 40s. The children of the third-wavers were usually grown by the time they immigrate; thus, these men are less concerned with material establishment—it is too late in their lives for that. Instead, they want to legitimate their role for their children and grandchildren so that they can remember their culture and remember the war and that the South Vietnamese were not just losers in this war. In their answers, they often recount their experiences in reeducation camp as proof of their victimization at the hands of the communists regime they left. For some, they describe reeducation camp in much richer detail than they do their wartime experiences. One man told me about his time in reeducation camp for 10 minutes without interruption.

All 40 men are, to varying degrees, anti-communist. Some of them do not think the war is not over, saying that they will continue fighting through an international network of émigrés to bring down the communist regime yet. "Even now," said Duy Nguyen, "though I am not in the army, and I don't have any weapons with me right now, but in my mind, I am against the communists, against the communists, against the communists."[34] Interviewing in the United States allows these men to speak about their experiences more freely, without fear of government censorship. Since these men are removed time-wise from the events, they may have forgotten or misremember details. Yet, being removed nearly 26 years from the experience of war and however many years from their release from reeducation camps allows the men to be more detached and can speak more candidly about their own mistakes, though many of these interviews were still

---

[34] Duy Nguyen, interview by author, San Jose, Calif., 24 June 2000.

emotionally-charged.

As I mentioned earlier, when I first began this project, I expected to hear the veterans tell me about the war from the perspective of subordinates to the Americans; I expected to hear a rejection of the tropes as to what happened. Therefore, in my early interviews, I invoked many of the dominant tropes found in the American representations in my line of questioning. A rejection of the dominant postwar American narrative requires accepting the terms on which it operates: the position of the RVNAF as subordinates. But most of them men did not see themselves as subordinates to the Americans they worked with. These interviews challenge the very premise on which previous narratives have been based. In their departure from the dominant interpretation of the war, these narratives are not just valuable because they come from an overlooked perspective, but because they are much richer and have more nuances than any told previously.

Approach to Interpretation: Need to Blame

As I mentioned earlier, my own research agenda is to find out what happened as opposed to why we lost, the question dominating postwar representations. This is not to suggest that the veterans share my agenda entirely, but that part of their desire to blame are reactions to tropes that function to answer that question. Almost every single veteran interviewed said that the America had "betrayed" and "abandoned" the RVN, marked by the Paris Treaty in 1973. Some even accuse the Americans with being "unfaithful allies." Not being "self-reliant" was the cause of the fall for South Vietnam, said Tran Duc Minh. "Don't rely too much on your allies, even though they are good ones. We are to blame for the loss of South Vietnam."[35]

The veterans cite Vietnamization as the impetus of the fall for RVN's struggle against the communists. America stopped supplying the RVNAF with equipment and ammunition, forcing the RVNAF to face the VC underequipped. "We were defeated not because we were not competent. We were competent to do the war," said Thanh Nguyen (Seattle). "But our hands were tied; we had no supplies."[36] Nghiem Hoa said, "I really hate how America helped South Vietnam for a long time, and then let South Vietnam lose the war. "[37] Others also felt a "total loss" from the American "betrayal." When America pulled out in 1973 under the Paris Treaty, they felt betrayed because the Americans had "broken their promise" to continue financial support after Vietnamization.

Although most of the veterans expressed varying degree of bitterness, most do not blame the Americans completely. When I asked them in the survey to explain the loss of the war, the men were divided between factors that placed blame on the Americans and factors that placed the blame on themselves, such as poor leadership in the RVN government. "Sometime we understand that our national leaders or high ranking officer don't know how to win the war....Even the South Vietnamese government didn't try what they have to try," Cam Nguyen said, who was much more anti-RVN government than the other veterans.[38] Duong Dien Nghi sometimes blames himself. "I was an officer over there, and at the time I was the

---

[35] Tran Duc Minh, interview by author, Redmond, Wash., 4 September 2000.

[36] Thanh Nguyen (Seattle), interview by author, Seattle, Wash., 26 August 2000. Because I interviewed another man by the name of Thanh Nguyen in Sacramento, I will indicate what Thanh Nguyen I am referring to in the text by location.

[37] Nghiem Hoa, interview by author, Seattle, Wash., 23 August 2000.

[38] Cam Nguyen, interview.

lieutenant colonel," he said. "I have a big responsibility for the loss and I knew it then."[39]

When the South Vietnamese veterans reinterpret these tropes, they sometimes dispute and sometimes agree with their meaning. Seldom do the individuals assert the tropes are unfounded. Most of them remember themselves as allies and equals to the Americans, not as subordinates. They dispute these tropes because they question the assumption of American paternalism; simultaneously, the veterans challenge the very purpose of these tropes in postwar American representations. Through these relatively candid interviews, many of the veterans reveal that they are more interested in telling their version of the Vietnam War and less in allocating blame. The veterans as individuals represent a wide spectrum in the process of blaming; some have moved passed blaming and have forgiven themselves and the Americans; others wanted to preserve a positive image of their role in the war.

American Paternalism

"Never did we consider Americans as our masters. We simply considered them our allies," said Tran Duc Minh, a colonel in the Army.[40] His words do not hint at resistance or bitterness towards his advisors as a subordinate. He describes his relationship with the Americans as he remembers it—it was one of equals. His words are echoed in the stories told to me by many other veterans. These veterans liken their relationship with their advisors, and the relationship between South Vietnam and America, to a partnership in which they had certain rights and the Americans had certain rights because of their individual

---

[39] Duong Dien Nghi, interview by author, San Jose, Calif., 14 July 2000.

[40] Tran Duc Minh, interview.

investments in the Vietnam War. Despite their differences, the veterans assert that they were allies who shared the same goal of fighting for freedom and democracy in Vietnam.

Naval commander Lam Dinh remembers when his advisor attempted to give more than just advice, Dinh would tell him, "You are aboard the ship as an advisor, please advise but I make the final decisions myself." If the advisors suggested something that Dinh thought would benefit the Vietnamese, he usually consented; if not, he would reject the advice. "Support is where they belonged," he said, "but commanding the force is our duty." He said he heard some units where the advisers also fought, but "if you know the rules, they cannot overpower you." The rules Dinh refers to are those of the military and those of the U.S.-RVNAF alliance. And regardless of how the men as individuals felt about these rules, they all understood their significance and complied with them.

The Americans, according to these veterans, also respected the Vietnamese. Dinh said that the advisers "really wanted to work with us, not against us." The Americans helped the Vietnamese with supplies, intelligence, and logistics, but when it came to operating the ship to battle or in fighting, Dinh said that, "I did the work, not them."[41] The role of the American advisor was to advise, not to command the RVNAF. The veterans usually believed that the Americans understood their place. The veterans did take the Americans' advice into account. "We respected each other and had a good relationship," Duong Ba said. "In each operation, we discussed procedures very carefully and shared ideas. I gave my opinion, they gave their opinions and we both decided together. That was good. But the decision was mine, not

---

[41] Lam Dinh, interview by author, Seattle, Wash., 24 August 2000. This is a pseudonym.

my advisor's."[42] This is not to say that the veterans never encountered patronizing advisors. When this happened, the veterans pointed to the military code of hierarchy. Dinh did differentiate between his experiences and those in the top ranks of the military, which he conceded the Americans controlled.

American paternalism seems so evident in the postwar representations, and yet most of the men who worked directly with advisors denied that the Americans were paternalistic. Instead, they emphasized the friendliness and mutual respect in their relationships. Some of them socialized outside in off-duty hours. Trang Van Do said he didn't know about other relationships, but he felt "very comfortable" with the Americans. They would come over to his house to sample Vietnamese food, including the smelly fish sauce, nước mắm.[43] Even those who did not work directly with the Americans had positive impressions of them. In 1976, a high ranking officer commented that "frictions and even head-on collisions" between advisors and ARVN commanders were "largely local and highly individual." He said that cooperation between advisors and counterparts were "close and since. The success of this productive relationship derived from two cardinal factors: self-respect and mutual respect."[44]

In contrast to what the GIs said in Full Metal Jacket, many of the veterans also sympathized with and appreciated the Americans, who they knew volunteered to come from a "rich country, to a poor country to face bad weather and the fight against communism." These sacrifices earned the respect of the Vietnamese. "Many of them were injured or died in the battlefield for us," said

---

[42] Duong Ba, interview by author, Seattle, Wash., 25 August 2000. This is a pseudonym.

[43] Trang Van Do, interview by author, San Jose, Calif., 20 July 2000.

[44] Hosmer, 43-44.

Kien Trong Truong.[45] "That's why we respect our alliance during the war." Sinh Le said that he knew the Americans had left behind "a wife, children, they have their own family, home"; with that in mind, he always tried to "protect them." When I asked why they thought their advisors respected them, most of the veterans cited that they needed them, and because they were fighting for shared ideals. Tuan Phan said that the Americans and the Vietnamese worked side-by-side, with the Americans relying on the guidance of the Vietnamese for survival because they were on "foreign turf."[46] "I know that Americans came to South Vietnam to fight for this ideal of freedom," said Le.[47] Many of the Vietnamese view the U.S. war effort in Vietnam as part of America's commitment to fighting the communists. Their views were not unlike the general Vietnamese population. In a 1971 survey of 478 Saigonese, 44 percent chose a favorable term to describe the Americans; 23 percent chose an unfavorable one; and the remaining third failed to comment. In the smaller cities of Dalat and Qui Nhon, significantly less of the population described the Americans negatively. Of those surveyed, 49 percent cited American aid as what they most liked about Americans.[48]

Not all the veterans had such positive memories of working with the Americans. The veterans who cited tense relationships tended to be those who were college-educated and generally more assimilated into American society. Sometimes the veterans felt that they were helping the Americans more than the Americans were helping

---

[45] Kien Trong Truong, interview by author, Seattle, Wash., 26 August 2000.

[46] Tuan Phan, interview by author, San Jose, Calif., 10 August 2000. This interview was done with a translator, another man named Tuan Phan.

[47] Sinh Le, interview by author, Sacramento, Calif., 23 July 2000.

[48] JUSPAO Survey/ Saigon. Public Opinion Survey, Jan 1971. Folder 102128, Box 80, National Archives, College Park, Maryland.

them.   Currently a college instructor, Thanh Nguyen (Sacramento) said of his advisors, "Some I liked, some I didn't like."   There was one American major in his company who often brought a gift of champagne or "something like that" to Nguyen, then a captain, every time he needed information.   "He's my advisor but he didn't know anything," Nguyen said with frustration.[49]

A self-described "trouble-maker," Thanh Nguyen (Seattle) said that he believed he was held back from promotion because of his disagreements with military policy regarding the Americans. He thought his advisors patronized the Vietnamese, smug with the knowledge that their country financially supported the RVNAF. "When I wanted anything for my division, there was no way for me to get it without the advisors," said Thanh Nguyen (Seattle), who now works in an American non-profit organization as a teacher. "They just had this power, and forced us to do what they wanted to do. They never listened to us. Even if they listened, it was, 'Oh, yeah, that's good idea' and after that, they did it their way." When he complained to his superior officers, they told him, "You blame the American; they are here to help us." Nguyen agreed that the Americans had come to help, but "I disagreed with the way they help us. They came to help us only. They cannot order us to do what they want us to do." Unlike many of his Vietnamese colleagues and superiors, Nguyen spoke both French and English fluently during the war and felt more conscious of what was happening. He did not accept the status quo as did his colleagues, who he said advanced much faster in the military hierarchy. He felt "very ashamed at that times" because of the incompetence of the RVN government and his superior officers as well as "American aggravation."[50]

---

[49] Thanh Nguyen (Sacramento), interview by author, Sacramento, Calif., 30 July 2000.

Another college-educated veteran, Anh Pham, was critical in his description of the American advisory effort, though he never personally worked with any advisors. In our conversation, I asked him what he thought about the American advisors:

JP: You call the Americans "advisors"...

TP: Well, they told us what to do that was good. They had the money, so you had to listen and do as they tell you.

JP: Did you feel that you were put in an inferior position to the Americans?

TP: Not inferior, but it was not friendly either.

JP: What kind of relationship would you compare it to?

TP: They're not the boss, but if you need help, you need to accept their...well, they are advisors. We called them advisors.

JP: So you felt you had to listen to what they said?

TP: Yeah, listen. But they were not colonizers, though they had power.[51]

When I pressed further to try to understand what he meant by "power," he retreated from the discussion, saying he seldom worked with the Americans himself. Having come in 1980, Pham has also lived in the United

---

[50] Thanh Nguyen (Seattle), interview.

[51] Anh Pham, interview by author, Seattle, Wash., 27 March 1999. This is a pseudonym.

34

States much longer than many of the other veterans I interviewed. He may have internalized the American discourse or felt more comfortable to express his genuine feelings, which happen to coincide with assumption of American paternalism. Those who immigrated in the third wave were generally more positive about their relationships with American advisors than those who had come in earlier waves.

Another aspect of American paternalism is racism. Postwar representations show us how Americans' paternalistic attitudes emerge in their racist language; the Americans see the Vietnamese as "gooks" and "chinks" rather than as people. Surprisingly, the vast majority of the veterans claim that the Americans they knew were not racist in their attitudes. Even those who never worked directly with Americans did not see them as racist. Thanh Nguyen (Seattle), who described the Americans as paternalistic, said that the advisors were not racist, except for two or three individuals.[52] Only a handful of people admitted to even feeling any racial tension. Kim Truong said that the racism from the Americans was subtle, but "When you look in their eyes, they don't have to say anything. It's the way they look at you."[53] For the most part, the RVNAF remembered the Americans fighting on the same side as they were; they were united by the same ideals, not divided by racism.

Since racism is so integral to the supposed subordination of the South Vietnamese, its absence in the veterans' narratives is remarkable and must be examined. If a veteran said he did not experience racism, I asked him to explain why this was the case. Most of them emphasized the Americans needed their help and that they were equals. As to their reaction to American advisor

---

[52] Thanh Nguyen (Seattle), interview.

[53] Kim Truong, interview by author, Seattle, Wash., 22 March 1999. This is a pseudonym.

paternalism, many veterans cited respect for the military hierarchy to explain why no racism existed. Nga Tran said, "In the army, American or Vietnamese, we must obey, and have discipline. When we see a higher ranking officer, we salute him, regardless if he is American or Vietnamese."[54] Some of the veterans even answered that the Americans could not be racist by nature.[55]

Perhaps cultural differences prevent the veterans from understanding racism in the same way Westerners do. From my interviews, this possibility seems an unlikely explanation. Many of the veterans recounted their parents' struggle against the colonial French "civilizing mission." With my postinterview surveys, I tried to gauge what racism meant to these men by asking them if they considered the My Lai massacre motivated by racism, as many Americans understand it to be. Most of the men said "no" and the rest answered "don't know." Of those who said it was a not a racist act, they wrote in explanations such as "war is war" and "war make people crazy" and "this is what war is like." They ranked My Lai among the other causalities of war. It is probable that they did face what we would term racism, but considered it a part of war and not worth bringing to critical attention.[56] Moreover, the veterans could also be reluctant to accuse the Americans of racism now that they live in the United States. If they did face racism as we know it, its long-term effects on them must be insignificant if these veterans do not invoke American racism in remembering the war.

American racism and paternalism are fundamental to representing the RVNAF as subordinates in their relationship with the Americans; the veterans rejected both. In doing so, they are consciously or unconsciously

---

[54] Nga Tran, interview by author, Sacramento, Calif., 30 July 2000.

[55] Survey results.

[56] Survey results.

changing the way others can define them, suggesting that partnerships between whites and nonwhites do not necessarily mean a paternalizer-subordinate dichotomy exist, and that factors other than race and patriarchy should be considered in understanding American-South Vietnamese relationships.

The veterans may not remember racism then in Vietnam, but perhaps now in the United States they encounter it. During the war, the veterans were in the ethnic majority; now they are in the minority. When I asked about American racism, third wave immigrant Nga Tran responded, "No, never in Vietnam, but here, I don't know exactly."[57] His hesitation perhaps points to how Vietnamese ethnicity, a reminder of a war Americans long to forget, is just another barrier to integration into mainstream American culture.

Vietnamese Apathy

"We didn't see a future after we graduated from high school," said Thanh Nguyen (Seattle). "People like me don't have connections. We have to join the army because we have to survive. There was no other way for you to survive." By the time Nguyen was a teenager, he said understood how bad communism was, but he still dreaded the prospect of spending his life in army. He knew that once men joined the army, they were there "forever, with no future, there was nothing for us.... I just wanted to be myself."[58] If Nguyen sounds apathetic toward the war effort, it is because he had the dreams and hopes typical of any young free man of military draft age anywhere. For most of the men, the military was their first and only

---

[57] Nga Tran, interview.

[58] Thanh Nguyen (Seattle), interview.

employer in Vietnam because the war lasted so long and began so early. Viewing Nguyen and the RVNAF as just subordinates denies them even the possibility of having the agency to want to form identities outside of their role in the military.

Despite the allusions by American postwar representations, apathy does not necessarily stem from lack of desire to fight or lack of patriotism. The apathy these men describe is not as one-dimensional as in the American representations. Even wartime American writers cite the duration of the war as explaining for this apathy; the explanation is lost in postwar representations.[59] The many facets of this apathy corresponds with the multitude of ways of coming to understand the meaning of the war and of communism as well with the individual aspirations of the veterans themselves. The sheer duration of the war explains some of the apathy, but the variety of stories show that apathy can be traced a web of factors.

About half the men interviewed admitted that they did not really comprehend the "reality of communism" until they served time in reeducation camp. Some men admit that while they knew it was their duty to join the RVNAF, they dreaded the idea of going into the military because they did not really understand what they were fighting. Many said that their parents never discussed politics as they were growing up; their understanding of the war was limited to "The South is fighting for freedom."[60] Neither did they feel the schools or the RVN government provided adequate education on communism to the general public. Therefore, the men were responsible for figuring out on their own what "communism" and "war" meant. "They

---

[59] For a more in-depth study of wartime representations in newsmagazines, see Julie Pham, "White Man's Burden to White Man's Guilt: Tracing the Epistemic Roots of Our Understanding of the ARVN," Undergraduate Thesis. UC Berkeley, Spring 2000.

[60] Survey results.

didn't show how bad the communists are," said Kien Trong Truong. "That's why the ideology, the policy against communists is not clear because citizens don't understand why we were against them. That's why in the war when the government ask the villagers to fight against communists, but the guerilla come every night, come everywhere, and talk to the villagers, share with them very nice things, lying words, sweet words, and the villagers were surprised and wondered why government asked them to be against communists."[61] As the war progressed, the recruiting efforts became significantly heavier. Recruiting meant "recruiting everyone, even those uncertain about their own beliefs in a war of ideologies." With little ideological motivation and material incentive, Khuyen said that "most service men saw nothing bright about their future in the military."[62]

Even once they began serving in the RVNAF, some men said they were attracted to the communist ideology. As traditionally is the case, intellectuals were attracted more often to communism. Bao Quoc Pham was 26 years old and a high school philosophy teacher when he was drafted. "At the time, I was very confused. I thought communism and nationalism were linked. I liked Marxism," he said. His family was one of the many who moved from the North to the South, and in the North his father had been a member of the Viet Minh, which influenced his attitude. Supporting the Viet Minh was not unusual among these veterans' families; 10 out 38 surveyed said parents had done so in the early years, when the Viet Minh was largely an anti-French group.[63] Old conflicted loyalties also explains the roots of ambivalence. In 1970, he joined the ARVN division assigned to writing the

---

[61] Kien Trong Truong, interview.

[62] Khuyen,153.

[63] Survey results.

military history. Surrounded by other intellectuals, he slowly debated his beliefs on communism. It was in this less emotionally heated arena that he changed his opinion by 1973. "I discovered that it was a big lie," he said. "Communism has two attitudes, but there is a contradiction in having nationalism and communism together. The communist element is then stronger."[64]

Tran Ngoc Phong had grown up in a strongly anti-communist household. His father had been jailed by the communists for one year when the family lived in North Vietnam before moving south in 1954. When he was seven years old, he said that he realized that the "Communists were the enemy and we fight against the enemy to weaken them and to destroy them." His father wanted him to study political science at the college level; Phong remembers him saying, "You must learn political science because you have to oppose the communists." At Da Lat University, Phong became exposed to different ways of this thinking and he began to reconsider his anticommunists stance. He told his father, "Don't worry about the communists. The communists now will be different from those before." His father became angry and said, "You study political science and you are stupid like a dog. Communists will never change." As an RVNAF instructor at Da Lat Academy, Phong was known as a liberal teacher who would sometimes disobeyed his superiors. His whole family was anticommunist; he alone had doubts. Only after reeducation camp did Phong realized his father was right. "I was stupid; the communists will never change," he said.[65] His words are echoed in others who admitted an attraction to communism that was only quelled by serving in reeducation camps. While ambivalence was more

---

[64] Bao Quoc Pham, interview.

[65] Tran Ngoc Phong, interview by author, San Jose, Calif., 9 August 2000.

prevalent among college educated, I stress that being college educated did not necessarily lead to ambivalence.

Tran Quoc Phong and Bao Quoc Pham are both from the North, but they were still young when they immigrated to South Vietnam. Some of the oldest veterans who were refugees from the North remembered life under communism more acutely; when they joined the RVNAF, they had no doubts as to where they stood on communism. They felt neither ambivalent or apathetic toward their cause, though they remember native Southerners questioning their motives for moving South and for fighting communism. These Northern refugees felt that they were even more patriotic than the native Southerners because of their contact with the communists and because the South Vietnamese government did not spend enough of their efforts on educating their citizens on the evils of communism.

Lam Dinh was 16 years old when he left the North. He remembers when he first came to the South, the Southern Vietnamese resented the presence of the Northerners, in part because the Southerners wanted to be reunified with the North. Dinh faced questions like: "Why you guys move down from the North to the South? The country has a chance to be reunited, why did you move down?" and "Why? We kicked the French out of the North and the French move to the South and the North would have kicked the French out of the South. Why did the Vietnamese from the North move to the South?" He remembers being discriminated against by Southerners in school for his Northern Vietnamese background that his tiếng Bắc [northern] accent betrayed. "The people who moved from the North to the South, they understand communism," said Dinh, "but the people in the South do not know it. They don't believe it." He said when he first joined the military, those in his company were overwhelming Northern refugees; he reasoned that the Southerners did not want to have a military that would further divide the North and South. Once in the navy though, Southerners and Northerners did not discriminate against each other because they had volunteered to fight for the same cause, much in the same way many of the veterans felt about the Americans advising in Vietnam. Referring to Northerners, he said, "We have to fight for freedom. If we don't join, who would join? The Southerners would not do it, they did not believe that the North is communist."[66] In truth, many of the veterans did not remember or tell me about any tensions between the native Southerners and Northern refugees.

Anticommunism was not the only attraction to joining the RVNAF. Army commander Vick Van Loc disagrees with anticommunism being a motivating force. A Northerner, Loc said that he joined the RVNAF in 1950 for career reasons. Becoming an officer at that time allowed social mobility, and he entered the "fancy" Da Lat Academy, the Vietnamese equivalent of West Point. Although he wanted to be a "lawyer or doctor or something like that," Loc knew that he would eventually be drafted into the military, so he volunteered. He does not believe veterans who cite patriotism or anticommunism as the reasons for joining the RVNAF because they are not politically conscious at that age. "Unless people make up stories to brag, most people of my generation don't really feel that way," said Loc. "When you are under 18 years old, you see something happen, it happens...So the political consciousness develops later." Loc grew up in the city in North Vietnam and had no negative experiences with the communists or the French. He moved his mother and siblings to the South in 1950 when he joined the RVNAF, not in 1954 with the mass exodus. When I asked why he chose the RVNAF instead of the North Vietnamese army if he felt ambivalent, he said that Da Lat Academy and a career officer's life was a

---

[66] Lam Dinh, interview.

"very good way for a young man." His apathy is not surprising considering Loc had no early experiences with communism and had escaped Vietnam in 1975, avoiding reeducation camp. Moreover, RVN ideological indoctrination began only after South Vietnam became a republic in 1955; he joined when many fought "with no conviction."[67] His anticommunism now is much quieter than many of his fellow émigrés. "I do hate the communists a little," he said, "but I don't want to pass my hate to the young generation."[68]

Many of the Southerners did say they grew up ambivalent about communism. When he was 14 years old, Thanh Nguyen (Seattle) witnessed his fellow native Southerners discriminate against the Northern refugees. He remembers them saying, "Oh, the Northerners are trying to gain land in the South. They say bad about communism, but things like that never happen like that." The Northerners came to South Vietnam with horror stories that many Southerners could not comprehend. Nguyen said he came to believe what "South Vietnam would never believe." In retrospect, many native Southerners wished the RVN government had indoctrinated the native population with more anti-communism. Thanh Nguyen said, "That was part of the mistake of South Vietnam. They never popularize the idea to fight against the communists. They didn't tell the South Vietnamese what the communists were really like."[69]

Aside from ambivalence toward communism, many felt that the war was just a "a fact of life." For Southerners, and particularly for those who joined in the second and third wave, the war had been going on for so long, the

---

[67] Khuyen, 253.

[68] Vinh Loc, interview by author, San Jose, Calif.,25 July 2000. This is a pseudonym.

[69] Thanh Nguyen (Seattle), interview.

specifics of the ideologies at war had been lost. Some just knew they were fighting for an ideal called freedom. "When I joined the army, I was fighting for freedom, I fight for peace between North and South," Loc Tran said. "Someone said, 'Maybe we are fighting for the Americans. And North Vietnam is fighting for Soviet Union'...But I don't think like that. Freedom is just freedom. I joined the army, I fought for freedom, I didn't fight for others— because they are not Vietnamese."[70] A pacifist by rearing, Minh Phan agreed with Tran. Minh Phan knew the communists "were very cruel," but he said, "we don't want die for ideologues. We don't believe in dying for communists or capitalism...I might fight, maybe, to defend my country, my people, my home, my family, my loved ones, but not for a doctrine."[71] Another man said that he felt at times the war was a "big game." These words reflects two dominant strains in the Vietnamese political consciousness: 1) a feeling that the RVNAF were sandwiched between two ideologies, communism and capitalism and 2) regardless of loyalty to either ideology, the men were fighting what they considered freedom for the Vietnamese. There was not the sense that this was a proxy war and the RVNAF was a mercenary force for the Americans. They just happened to share the same core values as the Americans.

Exhaustion and homesickness also contributed to apathy. Of the veterans surveyed, 63 percent said that when they joined the RVNAF, they thought the war would go on for a "long time, but not as long as it did" and "I thought it would never end."[72] The rest thought that the war would end quickly. Depending on the officers'

---

[70] Loc Tran, interview by author, San Jose, Calif.,21 September 2000.

[71] Geroge Phan, interview by author, Milpitas, Calif.,21 September 2000. This is a pseudonym.

[72] Survey results.

location, some saw their family for only one weekend every six months in contrast to the Americans, who went on R & R much more frequently. In Apocalypse Now, Captain Willard (Martin Sheen) comments on Charlie's content with "rat meat and cold rice" for R & R.[73] This description is then contrasted to the wild, pleasure island provided for the Americans. Yet the film overlooks how South Vietnamese lived or rested; indeed the RVNAF perspective is ignored almost completely throughout the film. Loc Tran was one of several commanders I interviewed who admitted that they boosted the morale of the men in their units by granting a few extra days of vacation, illegal by RVNAF standards. Tran saw his men as part of his extended family, and he knew they wanted to see their own families. His superior officer told him, "You cannot let your people visit their families, okay?" Although Tran would respond in the affirmative, he actually disobeyed his orders and would rotate 20 men out of 120 to let them visit their families. "My boss didn't like it and he said, 'Why you do that?' and I say I do that because I want to do that," said Tran. He explained that the superior officer could go home anytime he wanted, but his soldiers did not have the same privileges, "But they need to visit too; so I let them go." He understood that these men had concerns outside the military. Tran's story exemplifies war at the individual level, where decisions are made based on emotions rather than policy, and that what is seen as apathy toward the war can also be interpreted as a longing for civilian life.[74]

Another argument against the RVNAF with the apathy trope is that the Americans fought for the South Vietnamese, giving up their "own freedom to the gookers,"[75] who did not care enough about the war effort

---

[73] Apocalypse Now.

[74] Loc Tran, interview.

to do the job themselves. One veteran generally agreed with this statement. In my discussion with Vinh Loc, he told me:

> VL: Well, the South Vietnamese thought, "Okay, you come over here, you take care of hard job. You will be here for a year, no more, no less. When you go, we stay behind. We have to live with this war for the rest of our life. We are not in a hurry."

> JP: So did you think the mentality of the American was to come in, win and then leave? But with the Vietnamese, you think there was no hurry, they'd continue fighting the war?

> VL: For most Vietnamese, we know that there is no end to this game. So why get killed? Take it easy. The Americans are more than welcome to get into battlefield, do the hard work. That's the Vietnamese thinking when the Americans were in Vietnam.

> JP: And a lot of people you know thought this way?

> VL: Yes.[76]

Survival, not glory, motivated these men in battle. Van Phan agreed that the Americans were not so concerned with surviving because "they just have to fight one or two years and then they leave."[77] This fundamental difference in the duration of the tours explained why the Americans

---

[75] Full Metal Jacket.

[76] Vinh Loc, interview.

[77] Van Phan, interview by author, Seattle, Wash., 23 March 1999. This is a pseudonym.

were urgent and the Vietnamese were not, a distinction lost in postwar representations. Most of the RVNAF grew up with the war and never knew what peace time was like. For these men, the war was not a "big joke"; they were pawns in a game between two ideological blocs.

The veterans themselves did not deny that they felt an apathy and ambivalence toward the war effort. The Americans may have resented the Vietnamese for their apathy, but the Vietnamese, at a certain level, resented the war effort for denying them opportunities to pursue their own dreams and resented the Americans then for their resentment when they knew the Americans could return home and resume life outside the war. Gauging from postwar representations, these veterans feel that some Americans still do not sympathize with the South Vietnamese for what the Americans should understand fundamentally—the sacrifice of individual freedom for the collective freedom of their country. Through the South Vietnamese perspective, we can see that how the veterans are expressing their apathy in terms that the Americans themselves might invoke in describing themselves if they were in the same situation of participating a multi-decade war with no foreseeable end. One GI in Full Metal Jacket said that he felt his freedom had been taken away; some of these RVNAF men, for various reasons, would say the same thing.

The South Vietnamese see their apathy as a reasonable condition of war; the Americans see RVNAF apathy as contributing to the loss of the war. A reader of these narratives may speculate that these veterans are expressing their disempowerment and then conclude that the Americans have disempowered the South Vietnamese by imposing an unwanted war. But the apathy that these men describe stems not from lack of desire to fight or a lack of patriotism so much as the desire to have a normal civilian life, to, as a young man, have the possibility of having a future outside the military. They do not see the Americans as forcing this war on them; the war was a reaction to the Communists' "invasion" South Vietnam with its guerrilla agents. "The communists don't have the right to invade South Vietnam," said Nhuong Nguyen. "I know when people live under the control of the communists, they have no freedom, no democracy. So I joined the army to fight, to fight for freedom, for democracy, for South Vietnam."[78]

There is a motto in the RVVAF: "Duty, Honor, Country." When I surveyed these men as to what they considered the most important, 69 percent answered "duty" or "country." Another 17 percent said all three matter and 14 percent said honor.[79] "Without country, how can we have honor or duty? We lose our country now, what is the use of honor or duty without a country to serve?" said Tran Duc Minh. Though a minority of these men willingly volunteered for the RVNAF, most of them said they loved South Vietnam and had to defend their country. Tran felt a sense of resignation when he received his draft notice, but he said, "I am realistic enough to know that I had to ... stay in the army to fight the communists, if I wanted to be a free man in the South. There was no other way."[80]

Despite some ambivalence, RVNAF willingness to fight emerges in discussions of Vietnamization. Almost all of the men agree that Vietnamization would be acceptable if America had just pulled American troops, who contributed to the communist propaganda that America was colonizing South Vietnam. The veterans had supported Vietnamization of troops, but they said they still needed American funding. When this funding dwindled, many of the veterans felt that the Americans had "broken their promise." The veterans all admit to their financial

---

[78] Nhuong Nguyen, interview by author, Sacramento, Calif.,30 July 2000.

[79] Survey results.

[80] Tran Duc Minh, interivew.

dependence on American money. Duong Ba said, "They said they would give us the money and the weapon to fight, but they didn't do it, they didn't keep their promise."[81] "Guns without ammunition—what could we do?" asked Thanh Nguyen (Seattle).[82] Although "leading [South Vietnamese] personalities" did not like Vietnamization, most of the men approved of pulling American troops out of Vietnam as long as they still received financial support.[83] Only three out of 20 responses thought the American troops were necessary.[84] But they saw that financial support as part of a promise that America made to Vietnam in their mutual fight for democracy and freedom. In that fight, the South Vietnamese stayed and the Americans "abandoned" them.

Even though many of the men admitted that they did not want to go to war, they understood that it was their duty. The RVNAF had notoriously high desertion rates. Many of these veterans seem to shun those who shunned their duty. "I think those people, what they did are wrong to leave the country. You have to be responsible to protect your country and to obey the law and if there is some reason why can't be in Army or Air Force or Navy, it should be a good reason," said Can Tran, who was generally apathetic about his experience.[85] Loc Tran's own brother had forged his parents' signatures so that he could become a Ranger before draft age. Loc's father told him, "'I don't want you to run away. If you are needed, you go. But I don't want you guys volunteer.'"[86] While Tuan

---

81 Duong Ba, interview.

82 Thanh Nguyen (Seattle), interview.

83 Hosmer, 20.

84 Survey results.

85 Can Tran, interview.

Pham said he hated "cowards," he did not feel that it was his place to judge those who dodged the draft because of familial duties.[87]   Only Minh Phan admitted to that his family tried to get his younger brother out of serving for the RVNAF. He believed that almost everyone who was drafted wanted to avoid the draft. "If they don't admit this to you, they are lying," said Phan. "There are only 10 percent of men who want to fight, who are very aggressive, want to kill people. There are some people there who just want to fight no matter what they are fighting and they volunteer. Who want to die for a doctrine, for a philosophy?"[88]

Vietnamese Incompetence

The tropes itself both reinforces the subordinate position in terms of being the object of American paternalistic remarks in regards to incompetence, and give a reason as to why the RVNAF deserve to be put in the subordinate position in the first place. So, asking the veterans if they considered themselves competent is a highly subjective question, especially since statistical evidence shows that the many ARVN battalions were less successful than Americans ones in kill ratio.[89]   Instead, I asked how they compared the military competence of their advisors to their own performance. In a discussion with Vinh Loc, he talked about how experience factored into his working relationship with his advisors:

---

[86] Loc Tran, interview.

[87] Tuan Phan, interview.

[88] Minh Phan, interview.

[89] In late 1966, the ARVN battalions killed an average of 1.8 enemy soldiers per week; the U.S. battalions killed 8.6. (Clodfelter, 79).

JP: Did you feel that you were learning more from the Americans or they were learning more from you or equal?

VL: They are learning more from us.

JP: Why do you say that?

VL: Because they were here for only one or two years. They were always new in the country, but one after another, they left. The second guy might be the same as the first guy.

JP: What did you teach them about?

VL: We taught them about the war, the culture. They do know a little about the technical, how to organize, but they don't know how to apply the situation. But I myself learn from them, we know how to apply their technical, their money, their weapon to the war we live every day.

JP: When you went out into battle, did you feel like they were following you or you were following them?

VL: In my case, they had to follow me.[90]

Emergent in this discussion is how the veterans remember their experience level in comparison to their advisors, and how field experience made them equally, if not more competent, than the Americans. Loc makes several points about the advisor-counterpart relationship: 1) the Americans were more knowledgeable about logistics

---

[90] Tran Duc Minh, interview.

and technology; 2) the Vietnamese had more field experience; and 3) the Americans and Vietnamese worked together. Loc's experience is particularly akin to veterans who joined the war effort in the first wave. Except for the few career officers who served in Korea, most of the early U.S. Army company-grade officers assigned to field advisory duties has no real combat experience.[91]

In response to charges of incompetence, the veterans described a process of decision making in which the advisor advised and the counterpart could accept or reject that advice. In the process, they shared ideas and traded stories drawing from individual experiences before the RVNAF counterpart made the final decision. The Americans respected them for field experience; the Vietnamese looked to the Americans for logistical support. There was a partnership—an exchange of expertise—one in which both partners were competent in different areas. They relied on each other's competence in their respective expertise area to fight the war. This process occurred in the field, in pacification, in logistical support, in every Division of the RVNAF.

Comments similar to Vinh Loc were expressed by those I interviewed who worked with Americans mainly in field fighting units. Since he had been in the field since 1953, Tran Minh Duc said that the advisors "definitely" learned from him. But the advisors helped in other capacities, such as communicating with other Americans. "And in some areas, we do need their advice," said Tran Minh Duc. "For example, the Americans are coming, they're coming, they ask a lot of questions and sometimes our officers cannot express themselves, their opinions, their ideas. So we do need the American advisers to clarify the situation."[92] With logistics, the Americans were able to

---

[91] Khuyen, 74.

[92] Tran Duc Minh, interview.

assist the Vietnamese because they had more experience with the technology, or in Nga Tran's company, sophisticated information system. Tran spoke glowingly of his advisor, "He helped me with everything, he taught me everything he knew."[93] The counterparts were "gratified" that advisors helped with logistics and provided support.[94]

As this trope usually invokes a juxtaposition of the RVNAF competence to the ruthless capabilities of the Vietnamese communists, the charge of incompetence is an attack on the Vietnamese-ness of the RVNAF themselves. In my early interviews, I asked the veterans to compare RVNAF performance to the Vietnamese Communists. They responded by describing the motivation behind the Vietnamese communists. Peter Truong said, "I felt sorry for them because they were victimized by their own government. South Vietnamese soldiers are at least 18, but the North Vietnamese were sometimes only 14 or 15. They are forced to go and kill. They have no choice."[95] Again and again, their anticommunist sentiments as émigrés emerged. The communists "don't care about people. They allowed young boys to be chained to tanks and fight," said Binh Tran.[96] Several veterans compared the Vietnamese communists fighters to machines. But with the discipline came sacrifice. "There is a lot of discipline, but discipline in a way that forces people in the north to be tied to anti-aircraft machines and chained guns. As long as the gun was still working, they have to keep firing until they died," said Nhan Do.[97] Implicit in

---

[93] Nga Tran, interview.

[94] Gen. Cao Van Vien, et. al, *The U.S. Adviser*, Indochina Monograph (Washington, D.C.: U.S. Army Center of Military History, 1980), 68.

[95] Cao Truong, interview.

[96] Binh Tran, interview by author, Seattle, Wash., 25 March 1999. This is a pseudonym.

these stories is how the Communists government treats its people as opposed to the RVN government, and how this kind of cruel treatment is what they are fighting.

Their defensive reactions to this particular trope may be interpreted as them trying to reverse the blame for the loss of the war. In general, those who joined the RVNAF in the first wave seem to be more self-assured of their competence and equality with the Americans; those in the second and third wave were more ambiguous in their responses. "Like every army in the world, there are some good units and some bad units," said Duong Ba, who joined in 1964. "I cannot lie and say we are beating the communists. Sometimes we lost and we have to run away."[98]

Vietnamese Corruption

"Soldiers are soldiers. We were paid barely enough to live on and sometimes people were forced to steal," said Van Phan nonchalantly, justifying the charge of corruption against the RVNAF.[99] Kim Truong compared the situation of the Vietnamese to the Americans, who were well paid and could look "forward to serving in the military." "In Vietnam, the monthly salary only covers three to four days, so the RVNAF have to make up the rest and they have to be corrupt, so that is kind of bad," he said. The result of this corruption are soldiers who do not respect their commanders but "the commanders have their family, their children to feed too...When they sell to the enemy, they didn't think that indirectly, they were killing their family soldiers."[100]

---

[97] Nhan Do, interview.

[98] Duong Ba, interview.

[99] Van Phan, interview.

It was not until 1965 that corruption became a rampant problem in the RVNAF. But for the next five years, military leaders made anticorruption efforts one of their top priorities. The upswing in corruption is linked to the skyrocketing inflation. In 1964, an RVNAF colonel could make $400 a month, in 1972, his salary was worth $82 a month. A captain made $287 a month in 1964; by 1972, he made $61.[101] By 1973, no service man could live on his salary alone. Income rose fewer than three times for officers during 1964-1972 while consumer prices rose 8.5 times and rice 14 times.[102] Khuyen said the RVNAF man often had to make one of two humiliating choices: asking for financial support from their relatives or stealing from the military. "They knew it was wrong, yet their quest for survival seemed to be stronger than any sense of moral uprightousness," said Khuyen.[103]

The trope of corruption among the RVNAF functions to preserve the moral purity of Americans and to place the blame on the South Vietnamese, who supposedly took advantage of American financial generosity and whose avarice led to their self-destruction. Since rampant corruption is well documented, I worded my questions with the assumption that corruption did exist.[104] Almost all the veterans were willing to admit that corruption existed in the RVNAF, though few said they witnessed it themselves. Corruption, just like competence, is a highly

---

[100] Kim Truong, interview.

[101] Khuyen, 252.

[102] Ibid., 236.

[103] Ibid., 253.

[104] For examples, see Kim Do and Julie Kane, *Counterpart: a South Vietnamese Naval Officer's War* (Annapolis, MD: Naval Institute Press, 1998); Nguyen Cao Ky, *Twenty Years and Twenty Days* (New York: Stein and Day, 1976).

subjective trope for the veterans to address. Not surprisingly, most of the people used rumors ("I heard of it, but never saw it myself") to admit to corruption. Corruption existed, but it occurred in the higher ranks of the military or in the paramilitary or in the government—anywhere but where they had the power to change it. Duong Dien Nghi, an intelligence officer with the Psychological Operations Warfare divisions, said that there was "ghost soldiers" (*linh ma*) in the Popular and Regional Forces, but "not too much I think...Very little."[105] In fact, linh ma was one of the biggest sources of corruption in the RVNAF.[106]

Many of the RVNAF officers, often emphasized that the corruption was "very little," and that corruption exists everywhere, not just with the RVNAF or in South Vietnam. One man made an analogy: "See your hand? Some fingers short, some long. Like a family, some children, some good, some bad and the army is the same way. But it's not the big reason to say that we lost our country because of that. Don't believe that. Don't say anything about corruption...We served our country well."[107] Duy Nguyen agreed, "Every nation, anywhere, has some people good and bad, but here almost all good people."[108] Only Con Gia Pham vehemently denied any corruption: "I don't know, but I never saw it happen. I don't listen to rumors, I don't spread rumors."[109] None of them said that corruption was particular to the RVNAF; it was present in

---

[105] Duong Dien Nghi, interview.

[106] Khuyen.

[107] Anonymous, interview by author. This man is marked by his real name throughout the rest of the paper, but because of the nature of his comment, I decided this particular quote should be anonymous.

[108] Duy Nguyen, interview.

[109] Con Gia Pham, interview.

the U.S. Armed Forces also. Interestedly, none of these three men also participated in direct combat, perhaps explaining why they did not feel the effects of corruption so acutely.

Not all of the veterans were so nonchalant about the corruption in the RVNAF and its impact on the rest of the military. For those who did fight, corruption directly hurt them. Kien Trong Truong described how food, uniform, supplies, gas, oil, etc. were not sent directly to units; how *linh ma* were rampant, causing a shortage in soldiers that was "very painful to the people who were actually fighting. " I felt so bad about it because it directly affected us," said Truong. "I am a fighting officer; I have honor and responsibility to my country but no shoes for fighting. I have to spend my own money in black market for myself. How do the soldiers under me feel?"[110] From a high ranking officer's perspective, Lam Dinh said that the corruption in the high ranks directly affected the morale of the soldiers. The corruption did not compel people to revolt against their leaders, but they "kept quiet and lost trust, but still do job...People don't do well done job, just do a good job, but not well." It was difficult for soldiers to operate effectively, said Dinh, when supplies were being stolen by their own superiors.[111]

Without my prompting, some of the veterans describe the corruption of the current communist regime as being far worse. Duong Ba admitted that there was corruption during Thieu regime, but he said this corruption, in comparison to the corruption of the current regime, was like comparing "one dollar and one thousand dollars."[112] He converted my question into one that he felt comfortable answering, one that reinforces the

---

[110] Kien Trong Truong, interview.

[111] Lam Dinh, interview.

[112] Duong Ba, interview.

anticommunist stance of émigrés. This downplaying of RVNAF corruption as a contributing factor in the loss of the war could be a natural part of legitimization as a Vietnamese émigré. In the survey, I asked the veterans to circle the top three reasons they saw for the South Vietnamese loss of the war. "Corruption in South Vietnamese military" was circled just once; "corruption in South Vietnamese government" circled five times; "poor leadership in South Vietnamese government" circled 12 times; and "poor leadership in South Vietnamese military" circled five times. The top-rated reasons were "support from China, Russia to communist Vietnam" (14 votes) and "America abandoned support of Vietnam at that time" (18 votes).[113]

With the exception of a few people, most of the veterans admit to some degree of corruption in the RVNAF. At the same time, they ameliorate this corruption by pointing to corruption of the other participants in the war.

---

[113] Survey results.

ASSERTING VIETNAMESE-NESS IN AMERICA TODAY

"We are Vietnamese people, we are here not by choice. I would like to remind the younger generations, don't forget you are Vietnamese. Vietnam and the Vietnamese people still need you. We are proud to be Vietnamese," said Hung Pham, a second wave immigrant who was just a cadet officer at the fall of Saigon.[114] For many of these veterans, talking about the war is an assertion of their ties to Vietnam, despite having since immigrated to the United States. When asked on the survey if the veterans talked to their children about the war and if so, why, the overwhelming majority of them answered "yes" and that it was so that they could "remember their culture."[115] Like many of the other veterans, Pham hopes that one day the communist regime in Vietnam will collapse and that if they are still alive to see that day, they can return to Vietnam to at least visit.

---

[114] Hung Pham, interview by author, Milpitas, Calif., 15 August 2000. This is a pseudonym.

[115] Survey results.

Throughout my discussion of the tropes, I have pointed to how their usage depends on the assumption of an antagonistic relationship between the Americans and the South Vietnamese. The tropes of RVNAF apathy, incompetence, and corruption also invoke an implicit comparison to the North Vietnamese performance, and this comparisons suggests that the South Vietnamese are not as patriotic as their foes. In losing the war, the RVNAF also lost their country in the figurative and literal sense. RVNAF émigrés, in particular, are considered not as authentically Vietnamese because: 1) they allied with a Western nation and adapted to its ways during the war; 2) their vision of how Vietnam should be governed lost to that of the Vietnamese communists; and 3) they have since left Vietnam, arguably in pursuit of a more Western lifestyle.

In response to these tropes, these veterans continually assert that they were allies of the Americans, that they were fighting for the same ideals, and that they did so as Vietnamese patriots. Their identity is much more complicated than the paternalizer-subordinate dichotomy allows. "Remember me as a person, a Vietnamese, who loves Vietnam," said Can Tran in response to my question, "What do you want Americans and Vietnamese Americans to know about the South Vietnamese military role in the Vietnam War?"[116] There is a fear among these veterans that because their ideal of Vietnam lost, they might seem less "Vietnamese," less patriotic, than the Communists. As émigrés, that fear amplifies because they willingly left Vietnam to live in the West. Many of the émigrés said they left because they could not continue to live under a communist regime. This compulsion to escape Vietnam was especially true for those who had served time in reeducation camp, like Bui Do. "After camp, we had no freedom, no anything," he said. "I just wanted to find

---

[116] Can Tran, interview.

freedom...We come to the United States only to find freedom."[117]   When the fall of Saigon occurred, Than Chieu said that he felt like he lost everything, but he said now, "I believe as refugees here, life is better life here and we have more freedom than in South Vietnam."[118]   I asked the veterans how they felt about being in the United States now. Sixteen answered, "Good, I am glad I am here and not in Vietnam," followed by eight answering, "Good, I am glad I am here because I like American better than Vietnamese lifestyle."[119]   Others wrote in that they are happy to be in America for the sake of their children.

As Westernized as the South Vietnamese lifestyle was in comparison to the North, these men did not see themselves as the "Vietnamese surrogates" for the Americans.   They are simply themselves: Vietnamese nationals who recognize that their home is in America now, but that does not mean they have given up their Vietnamese core.   During the war, they did develop a dependance on American support, as attested by their protests to Vietnamization. Yet they were never jealous of the high living standards that the Americans carried with them to Vietnam.   Khuyen also noted this lack of jealousy.[120]

At the same time that these veterans are anti-communists, they remember the individual enemies with compassion. They recognize the communist soldiers and officers as their fellow countrymen who have just been "brainwashed." When I asked the veterans what they thought compelled the Vietnamese Communists to fight,

---

[117] Bui Do, interview by author, Seattle, Wash., 25 March 1999. This is a pseudonym.

[118] Than chieu, interview by author, Seattle, Wash., 3 September 2000. This is a pseudonym.

[119] Survey results.

[120] Khuyen.

11 men answered that the VC had to follow the communists because they lived in the North; another 11 thought that the VC were simply misled; and only a few people thought the VC followed the communist ideology out of choice.[121] Most of the RVNAF veterans did not necessarily hate the Communists soldiers as individual. They pitied the VC soldiers who did not realize that everything the Communists did and said was a "big lie." Ky Nguyen described an incident in which his company communicated with the Communists during a cease-fire in 1973. "We were in a valley separated by a small river, and we took turns talking through a horn. This communist soldier was telling us how everyone in the South was poor, and the police and the army were bad, but he didn't know that the south was free. He didn't know," Nguyen said. "Where I live in the South, it was very poor, very hungry. But there was freedom. We told him this."[122] Minh Phan reflected the sentiments of many of the men I interviewed when he said, "North and South are the same people. The North fight harder because they were forced to fight. They have no freedom to avoid fighting."[123] When the veterans compare themselves to the North Vietnamese/Communists, it is not in terms of apathy, corruption, or incompetence. It was not a matter of who was more "Vietnamese"; the veterans saw both sides being equally Vietnamese. Instead, the veterans reiterate that they were conscious of their individual freedom and the sacrifice of that freedom for a collective freedom; in contrast, the North Vietnamese lacked that consciousness.

I asked the veterans if they would ever go back to Vietnam, just to visit. The majority, 22 out of 28,

---

[121] Survey results.

[122] Ky Nguyen, interview by author, Seattle, Wash., 22 March 1999. This is a pseudonym.

[123] Minh Phan, interview.

answered in the negative. Many wrote in that they would not return until the communist regime had been overturned. One veteran, who came in 1994, wrote on the "other" option line, "I'm in the U.S. and I am a U.S. citizen, but I am still Vietnamese."[124] Third wave immigrant Song Nhi said that while he was happy to become an American citizen, he had not wanted to give up his Vietnamese citizenship in the process.[125] It was sacrifice they made for what they considered individual freedom.

---

[124] Survey results.

[125] Song Nhi, interview by author, San Jose., 23 August 2000.

CONCLUSION

I asked these veterans if they were aware of how they were portrayed in American representations, and if so, how did they feel about it. One veteran, Duong Ba, was particularly expressive:

DB: They have done this before, they do it now and they will continue in the future too. They do it, I don't know why but they still do it.

JP: Do what?

DB: Betray us. They stab us with a knife. They try to overturn history. They try to change black to white and white to black. I want Americans and Vietnamese Americans to know the truth and always the truth.

JP: What is the truth?

DB: We had the right to fight during the war because the North infiltrated to the South and we had responsibility to fight back against them. That is the truth. And I want future generations to know about it.[126]

For him, and for many other veterans, making black black again and white white again, is not just a matter of negating the tropes that define them. Instead, they want to share their side of the story, explain what happened in Vietnam, and to show that they fought in the war for freedom, democracy, love and duty toward their homeland along with, not for, the Americans. "We were fighting for people, for human rights," said Duy Nguyen. "We don't try to murder people. I just wanted to protect myself, my family, and my freedom. But some people think we fight for money, for something like that. That makes me feel really bad because it's not true."[127] They do not remember themselves as mercenaries in a proxy war, or as subordinates.

Twice betrayed by the Americans, these veterans said. First was when the Americans left them with no financial support to fight the North Vietnamese, who the Russians and Chinese backed. Although there is bitterness, many of the veterans seem to have forgiven or are on the path to forgiving the Americans on the first count. As allies, they share the blame for the loss. Bui Do said, "I don't blame the Americans. It is a shared responsibility between the American side, the Vietnamese side."[128] For Do and many others, they know they cannot change the past; they can

---

[126] Duong Ba, interview.

[127] Duy Nguyen, interview.

[128] Bui Do, interview.

only hope to change how the past is perceived.

The war over representations, over the second betrayal, is still being fought and has to do with how, as Duong Ba, said, "they continue to kill us." He refers to the negative portrayal of the South Vietnamese military as the fumbling sidekicks of the Americans and the lesser Vietnamese of the Vietnamese. The definition of the RVNAF rests on recycled tropes that themselves assume certain relationships to be universally true and certain questions to be considered unanimously important. The veterans feel betrayed not because the tropes are complete lies, but because they are never questioned, never nuanced, never explored. Americans unconsciously digest these representations, without trying to reconcile the Vietnamese Americans they know with the ones they see on the screen. The veterans themselves are divided over if they feel the Americans are yet sympathetic to the South Vietnamese military role in the Vietnam War, though there is consensus that the RVNAF have gained more respect in recent years,[129] as proven by recent apologies from celebrities like Joan Baez and Jane Fonda, former Communist sympathizers.[130] Their enemy is still the communists; they hope their allies are still the Americans. And though they all want to see the communist regime toppled, that there is still a war to be fought in that sense, they disagree over who will fight it, whether it be their generation who lets the bitterness swell or whether they pass it onto their children. Nhan Do said to me, "I'm too old, let your generation accomplish that."[131]

---

[129] Survey results: 13 agreed that Americans under, "but it has only ben in recent years that they have come to understand"; six offered no explanation, but just said "yes." Only four disagreed, because they feel the Americans still believe in negative media.

[130] David Hinckley, "Why we still care about Hanoi Jane," *Daily News* (New York) 25 June 25, 2000, Sunday sports final edition, *http://web.lexis-nexis.com/universe/document?* Accessed 18 April 2000.

Language skills and immigrant status have long prevented these men from publicizing these stories themselves; many saw me as a way to finally express their feelings. Just as there is a dialogue with changing the perception of the past, there is a hope that what they say will have an impact on the future. Their stories do not reject the American representations, perhaps because they are not exclusively Vietnamese stories. These stories are hybridized, told by Vietnamese American émigrés. Together, they comprise a new way of imagining the war and who was in it and what they were thinking and what they did. In this new narrative, the role of "ally" to the Americans replaces that of subordinate, the question of who is to blame is less central to the research agenda, and the RVNAF cease to be defined in relation to the Americans and the North Vietnamese.

At the end of one interview, Hung Pham told me, "In my dream, I can speak English well and very persuasively. I tell Americans a story, tell them about my perception, my view about the war and tell them why communism is not good for the country and communism is why the South Vietnamese people had to flee Vietnam in 1975 and that is why we are here now."[132]

I offer this research as a step toward fulfilling that dream.

---

[131] Nhan Do, interview.

[132] Hung Pham, interview.

Navy Admiral Chon Van Tran being interviewed by Julie Pham in San Jose. Admiral Tran talked about the South Vietnamese military and their relationship with Americans. Circa 1999.

Dr. Con Gia Pham (left) and Editor Quoc Bao Pham after being interviewed by Julie Pham in Seattle. Their conversation inspired *Their War*. Circa 2000.

INTERVIEWS BY JULIE PHAM

Tape recordings and transcripts within author's possession. All interviews are in English, unless otherwise noted.

*Name has been changed at interviewee's request.

Phan, George.* Milpitas, Ca. 21 September 2000.

Phan, Tuan. San Jose, Ca., 10 August 2000.

Pham, Tan. San Jose, Ca., 30 June 2000.

Pham, Ned. * San Jose, Ca., 15 August 2000.

Nguyen, Duy. Milpitas, Ca., 24 June 2000.

Tran, Loc. San Jose, Ca., 21 September 2000.

Nhi, Song. San Jose, Ca., 23 August 2000.

Do, Trang Van. San Jose, Ca., 20 July 2000.

Do, Nhan. San Jose, Ca., 11 August 2000.

Tran, Phong. San Jose, Ca., 8 August 2000.

Tran, Henry.* San Jose, Ca., 24 June 2000.

Nguyen, Nhuong. Sacramento, Ca., 30 July 2000.

Tran, Nga. Sacramento, Ca., 30 July 2000.

Le, Sinh. Sacramento, Ca., 23 July 2000.

Nguyen, Thanh. Sacramento, Ca., 30 July 2000.

Truong, John.* Seattle, Wa., 22 March 1999

Phan, Tom.* Seattle, Wa., 23 March 1999.

Do, Luke.* Seattle, Wa., 25 March 1999.

Pham, Bao Quoc. Seattle, Wa., 27 March 1999.

Truong, Pete.* Seattle, Wa., 22 March 1999.

Nguyen, Cameron.* Seattle, Wa., 22 March 1999.

Tran, Robert.* Seattle, Wa., 25 March 1999.

Pham, Con Gia. Seattle, Wa., 27 March 1999.

Pham, Ted.* Seattle, Wa., 27 March 1999.

Tran, Van.* Seattle, Wa., 24 March 1999.

Truong, Thong. Seattle, Wa., 23 August 2000.

Ba, Dirk.* Seattle, Wa., 25 August 2000.

Nguyen, Sam.* Seattle, Wa., 26 August 2000.

Chieu, Ted.* Seattle, Wa., 3 September 2000.

Hoa, Nghiem. Seattle, Wa.,23 August 2000.

Hung, Howard.* Seattle, Wa., 26 August 2000.

Dinh, Mark.* Seattle, Wa., 24 August 2000.

Nguyen, Thanh. Seattle, Wa., 26 August 2000.

Lu, Toan The. Seattle, Wa., 24 August 2000.

Minh, Tran Duc. Redmond, Wa., 4 September 2000.

Stephen T. Hosmer, Konrad Kellen, Brian M. Jenkins. The Fall of South Vietnam: Statements by South Vietnamese Military and Civilian Leaders. New York: Crane, Russak and Co., Inc. 1980

Nguyen Cao Ky Twenty Years and Twenty Days. New York: Stein and Day, 1976.

MY MEMORIES OF THE AUTHOR OF "THEIR WAR"

By Phạm Quốc Bảo
Translated by An Huynh

I went to Seattle for my personal business on the weekend from September 22 to 23, 2018. Kim Pham, founder of the Northwest Vietnamese News shared that he randomly found my "Ten Days Journey," published by Washington Viet News (owned by Giang Huu Tuyen) in 1987 when being busy preparing for his newspaper's classical music gathering event. He took the book off the family bookshelves, read it slowly, and we recalled how we felt about our road trip to the World Fair "Expo 86" Exhibition in Vancouver- BC, which was mentioned in the book.

He also commented that although the layout of the

book, from the cover illustrated by artist Nguyen Thi Hop and Nguyen Dong to the black and white pictures inside, did not meet today's printing standards, it was still very inspiring and emotional compared to many modern but soulless prints.

Looking Back Twenty Years Later

Kim reminded me of my seventh published book. During the summer in 1986, my wife and I did a road trip to North California with my youngest brother's family and another friend's family. We camped in Yosemite National Park after visiting my brother-in-law's big family in Pittsburg (close to Concord, a one-hour drive from San Jose). My wife decided to stay there for a few days while I flew to Seattle to visit my friends (mainly Kim's family) and Vancouver to attend the World Expo '86 Exhibition.

After settling down in the United States for several months, Pham Kim started working with Tran Thang – a musical producer. Tran Thang was the first Vietnamese in the United States to produce music shows like Hollywood Night at Fifth Ave Theater in 1983). These two guys worked together at a marine manufacturing plant in Tacoma. This company manufactured Naval Ships for the Vietnam War; and Washington State was the biggest plywood and Yakima apple exporter to Saigon before 1975.

Kim also owned a small printing shop, named South Vietnam Graphics Design -Stationery. This was one of a few printing shops owned by Vietnamese. At the time, it would have been difficult to publish a newspaper in this small Vietnamese community.

That was my first time going to an evergreen city with the clean and fresh air (compared to the polluted air quality in southern California) and a Vietnamese community numbered around 25,000 (in 1986). I was intrigued by all the exciting things about this new immigrant community finding their ways to grow. In spite of my short stay in Seattle, I kept writing passionately every night. My writing reflected my fresh sentiments about the sightseeing, the lifestyle in this city and the nostalgic feeling for all the memories in the past.

That's how I wrote the *"Ten Days Journey"* and published each chapter in the Vietnamese Newspaper in southern California (published three times per week) as well as the *Sinh Hoat Thuong Mai* in Seattle, published by Win Realty- real estate company and designed and printed by South Vietnam Graphics Design Printing.

From June to December 1986, Kim was supported by the Vietnamese Newspaper in southern California to launch the weekly newspaper - Northwest Vietnamese News.

At the launch of Northwest Vietnamese News, I met with the Vietnamese artist community in Pacific Northwest who joined the event: Doan Chau Mau, Huy Quang-Vu Duc Vinh, Tuy Hong, Quoc Lam, Cao Hoang, Do Huu Tuoc, Nguyen Van Nha, Do Huu Nho, Do Minh Duc, Tran Thien Hiep, Vu Quoc Thuy, Tran Thi Lai Hong, Le Phuoc Tho, Nguyen Phong, Bui Dinh Lieu, Nguyen Cong Khanh, Kim Long, Pham Van Minh, Nguyen Tan Lai, Thien Nhat Phuong, Mai Long, Lý Quốc Ngoc, Tran Khai, Tran Thang from Seattle, Nhat Tuan-Pham Hau, Ha Huyen Chi, Nguyen Tuong Thiet from Tacoma, Tu Cong Phung from Portland, Ha Quoc Bao from Richland.

One year later, in 1987, my book was published by the Washington Viet Post (owned by Giang Huu Tuyen) in Washington D.C. and launched in Seattle in the "Spring Art and Literature Night" at the University of Washington's Event Hall. The launch event was sponsored by the Vietnamese Student Union. (Nguyen Hung, the chairman at that time, has been practicing medical care for twenty-five years in Orange County). Doan Chau Mau gave the open speech, Huy Quang-Vu Duc Vinh and Doctor Nguyen Hy Vong introduced the book and author.

The show was performed by student singers: Tịnh Trang and friends, and Ha Quoc Bao (crossed 200 miles through the Cascades of Washington State), Tram Tu Thieng, Nhat Ngan and Tran Dinh Quan from South California.

In the last few months of 2007, Northwest Vietnamese News has gone through a long period of more than 20 years and currently published twice per week for a big Vietnamese community with a population of approximately 60,000 in Washington State, with a concentration in Seattle. However, the pioneers contributed to the newspaper in its very first days have passed away. The first one who left us is Quoc Lam, following by Doan Chau Mau in Hawaii. In this century, we lost Tram Tu Thieng, Tran Dinh Quan in Little Saigon, then Giang Huu Tuyen in Washington DC. Huy Quang-Vu Duc Vinh passed away last year and recently Nguyen Luong Thuat also left us in the middle of September 2017 at the age of 66.

And who else will leave us in the upcoming years? Who? No one of us can really tell!

Twenty years (1986 - 2006) - A generation

A nostalgic feeling arose in my heart once I looked back. It was a combination of appreciation, affection, and sorrow for those who passed away: the gentle smile of Huy Quang-Vu Duc Vinh, the heartfelt conversation of Quoc Lam, the loud voice of Doan Chau Mau, the happy laugh of Giang Huu Tuyen.

Then I thought of the peaceful face of Dr Le Phuoc Tho whom I haven't met for a year and the cheerful laugh of Ha Quoc Bao in our weekly call.

And in the middle of these emotion waves, I thought

about myself, the lonely self trying to balance between the past and the presence when life keeps passing me by.

*

On the other hand, I have hope for the younger generation who is extremely passionate, energetic and constantly pushing themselves moving forward. And of course, they will set new milestones for our community while the older generation, like my friends and myself, is reaching another stage of life.

In November 1986, I went back to Seattle to help Pham Kim to prepare for Northwest Vietnamese News publication. At that time, Kim's family rented an old house in Federal Way. We (Kim, his spouse, and friends from southern California) had been working all day long and only returned home for sleeping very late at night. A couple of weeks passed by, and I rarely had time to pay attention to Kim's children, including the oldest daughter, Julie and two younger sons, Andy and Bảo Don. I only know that they were studying at a kindergarten or elementary school near home. I sometimes saw them playing on the swings in the backyard on the weekends. On page 70 of "Ten Days Journey", I did mention them *"... When I stayed at their house, Nga and Kim changed their daily routine to accommodate me. Although their kids - the 9-year-old daughter and 7-year-old son - were on the summer break, they knew how to take care of themselves without letting their parents worry about them. And Nga could bring the youngest son - Bảo Don every time she wanted to leave the house".* In general, I only remembered them as those quiet shadows living upstairs. That's it.

When I returned to Seattle a couple years later, I sometimes saw Kim's kids in the car when Nga or Kim drove me to work. Sitting in the same car, we kept discussing about work and other stuff and I rarely had a chance to really talk to them.

At the end of the 1990s, Pham Kim let me know that Julie went to college at University of California, Berkeley. "She is looking for the documents about the Army of the Republic of Vietnam," he said. We immediately came up with a plan for Julie to interview directly the former members of the Army of the Republic of Vietnam. This research took place from southern California to Seattle in two years. We started with the Navy Admiral Tran Van Chon (San Jose) and even interviewed a veteran living on the East Coast of the United States.

Julie graduated magna cum laude from the University of California, Berkeley at the beginning of the twenty-first century and her research was included in the "Outstanding Undergraduate Research Showcase" at UC Berkeley that year.

In 2017, she earned her PhD in History at the University of Cambridge in the United Kingdom, and then taught History and managed the Journal of Vietnamese Studies at the University of California, Berkeley. What made me most proud was that Julie Pham Hoai Huong successfully guided her two siblings to complete their Bachelor's degrees. Andy Pham earned the CPA certification and Don Pham graduated from the University of Washington and is now working at Microsoft.

They have held important roles in managing the Vietnamese Northwest News and Dong Phuong also works there as a finance controller. They had started with the Yellow Pages Phone Book in 2007 and developed the online services. Paying attention to what they have been doing, I realized that they show their appreciation for all the hard work of the older generation by participating in the family business besides working for what they are passionate about. Supporting the family business is more about fulfilling their responsibilities than making profits.

This is the essential value of the young generation no matter which country they choose to live and work.

THE VIETNAM WAR: SEATTLE MAN RECALLS HIS STORY AS A VIETNAMESE OFFICER

By Kim Pham / September 25, 2017

First published by Crosscut Media:
https://crosscut.com/2017/09/vietnam-war-south-vietnamese-officer-perspective-democracy-communism

Before coming to the United States, Kim Pham was an officer in South Vietnam's navy during the Vietnam War. Here is his story, as told to his daughter Julie Pham. They came to Seattle as refugees from Vietnam in 1979.

The first time I was a refugee, I was 4 years old.

The First French Indochina War had already started by the time I was born in 1950 in Ninh Binh-Thanh Hoa, a heavily Catholic Northern province in Vietnam. When I was 4 years old, the Geneva Accord split the country in half and people could choose to migrate north or south.

Although I couldn't remember anything at that time because I was a child, my family told me the communists were terrorizing the north. Everyone was afraid of them. So when there was an opportunity for us to go south, we took it.

We eventually settled in Saigon. I went with my parents, my older sister, my older brother and my younger sister. Through family connections, my father got a great job working for USAID, an American news agency that published the beautiful magazine, Thế Giới Tự Do (The Freedom World).

I began to understand the concept of war when I was 10 years old as I started to recognize the fighting as warfare and from reading the USAID materials. I studied at Lasalle Taberd, one of the elite French-Vietnamese schools for boys in Saigon. My uncle, Frère Adrien Pham Ngoc Hoa, was the principal and one of founders of Lasalle University before 1975. When I was 16 years old, I started to really think about the war because being drafted was only a few years away.

All able men in South Vietnam were drafted. It was not a matter of if, but when.

We knew it was our responsibility to fight for freedom and democracy in the South. The other side was a dictatorship. They were coming from the North to the South and killing people. But we also knew that fighting for this freedom would likely mean sacrifice and death. Every day, I'd see the flags and coffins in the streets, people dying and crying and bombings. Just because we knew it was the right thing to do didn't make the prospect of death to an 18 or 19 year old any less scary.

Knowing how my scared my parents were, I studied hard at night and I took the test again. Being able to go into the officer corps was the difference between life and death. When you know you're about to die, you have to continue to push through. The second time, I passed.

The day I entered the military, my family was very sad. I felt like I was waiting to die, like I was someone with cancer. As a young man, I didn't know much about the world and all I could think about was dying. I knew fighting for the freedom of people in the South came with an expensive price — the cost of our lives. In war, we all wanted to do something courageous, but we also wanted to be away from danger as much as possible. I had friends who died.

Being an officer meant I could be stationed in Saigon. I could go home at night. I selected serving in the Navy. At the time, there were only two fields of study that military officers could take while also serving: Law and Humanities. The other fields would have required us to be there during the day. I went to law school starting in 1971. In the classroom, I met many other naval officers and my future wife.

Once I knew I'd been accepted as a naval officer, I worked to get accepted into the press corps, which was considered an honor. In high school, instead of music or sports, I chose to write and report part-time for a Saigon newspaper and it prepared me well.

As a press officer, I had to gain the trust of our readers and to prove we were right to fight the North. My job was to show people the horror of communism, so they would know that even if they died in war, it was for the right thing and an honor.

I loved my job. I read a lot and interviewed many people who were anti-communist. I also interviewed North soldiers who were prisoners of war, and I empathized with them. I knew their parents were also worried about them. When we met one-on-one, I didn't feel they were my enemies.

In early 1975, I got married. By that time, many troops from the North were invading the South. Saigon was chaotic at the time. There were bombings often, including suicide bombings. There were communist spies everywhere. They lived among us. There was a lot of fear and paranoia. I remember communists trying to trap the president of the law school.

Although there was terror in the streets, there was still a belief the Americans would protect us. I shared this faith that the Americans would save us with many other Southerners. Though they pulled out their troops in 1972, we believed they would still help us. We were all wrong.

By April, we knew the end was near. Many people wanted to get to the Navy ship, but the road from home to the port was destroyed. We had planned to leave on the morning of April 30, but we couldn't find a way. For us to have made it in time to the ship to escape Vietnam, we would have had to have gotten there the night before. By noon on April 30, 1975, Saigon fell. I was at the Navy headquarters, but my family was still at home.

We were one day too late. All the ships left straight for Guam. When it's time to sink a ship, the plug gets pulled and water fills the ship. I felt like I was a ship whose plug had been pulled out and I was sinking. That moment was so hard. Many committed suicide.

In the two months that followed the Fall of Saigon, everyone was selling their possessions like a big garage sale. Drawers, tables and all sorts of furniture were out on the streets. Newly wealthy communists were coming in and buying things from the Southerners.

Then all the South Vietnamese officers were rounded up by the Communist government and we were told we'd go to study for 10 days. We now refer to where we were taken as re-education camp. We were then put into a big Molotov trucks, covered with canvas. It was hard to breathe. We had to try to poke holes through the canvas to breathe. There were 40 people on each truck. It was an eight-hour ride. That was the start of prison.

Ten days became 15 days, then one month, and then we knew we had been cheated and lied to. It was very hard. We barely had any clothes or food and we slept on the ground. Every four to five months, we were moved to another site. Some committed suicide. My wife was allowed to visit every three to six months. The communists would send a letter out and give them a date and the site and they were allowed to bring a package no more than 10 kilograms [about 22 pounds]. They would get one hour to visit.

Every month or two, we would be forced to write down all the things we did wrong, and denounce people. For those who denounced a lot of people, they would be praised. They thought they would get to go home earlier, but they didn't. We held this hope the Americans would save us. Eventually, with the Humanitarian Operation resettlements, the United States did bring many former political prisoners and their families to America.

I was released after three years. I didn't trust anyone. I was afraid they were communists. But because I was afraid of being sent back, I found a way to pay for passage on a boat to escape. I fled from Vietnam in 1979 with you and your mother. We were the first ones in our family to leave. Coming to the U.S., I was a refugee for the second time in my life.

I haven't been back to Vietnam since. Thinking about Vietnam makes me feel so sad. Today, I am still a reporter serving my community. I started the Northwest Vietnamese News with your mother in 1986 in Seattle to serve Vietnamese people here in the Northwest.

I know there are many Americans who protested the war, and who still believe it was wrong. As a South Vietnamese officer who directly witnessed a lot of suffering, I believed then and I still believe we were fighting for what was right.

I've had unrealized dreams in my life. Northwest Vietnamese News gives voice to those who escaped Vietnam for the U.S. in search of the freedom and democracy we couldn't achieve at home.

ABOUT THE AUTHOR

Julie Pham graduated magna cum laude from the University of California, Berkeley in 2001 and earned her PhD in History at Cambridge University as a Gate Cambridge Scholar in 2008. Her parents founded Nguoi Viet Tay Bac, the largest Vietnamese newspaper in the Pacific Northwest, in 1986. Pham wrote "Their War" as her honors undergraduate thesis in history in 2001 with the support of the Haas Scholars Program.

CPSIA information can be obtained
at www.ICGtesting.com
Printed in the USA
LVHW090027041019
633169LV00001B/189/P